Converted

Uncover The Hidden Strategies You Need To Achieve Massive Credit Score Success

NATHALIE NOISETTE

Disclaimer:

All information within this book reflects the author's opinion in proximity to when the book was published. Credit and best practices are ever-changing organisms; due to this notion, there can be changes to this content at any time based on new information. Also, the author's opinion may change as well.

Again, these are opinions based on expert experience. The author has done their due diligence to ensure that the information presented is presented with the most relevant information but takes no responsibility for any changes made. You are more than welcome to cross-reference any information presented in this clip.

Any missing information is not the responsibility of the author. Any results, direct, indirect or consequential, or otherwise, are not the author's responsibility. The information is not a substitute for legal advice. If you need legal advice, please get in touch with a qualified attorney.

Dedication

This book is dedicated to my devoted mother.
Mom, the curse is broken.
We are free.

Acknowledgments

I want to acknowledge the many people that contributed to making this book a reality. First and foremost, thank you to my editor Larry Butler. This book would read very different without him. My daughter Alani, for coming into my life and kicking it into high gear. To my mother for her endless support and patience as I finished the book.

Then there is my family Gaelle, Jessica, Gesner, Nasha, Alain, and the countless friends that lent me their ears to work out ideas, encourage me to finish, and trust in the process.

Lastly, to my dear clients for trusting my guidance through the years. Their trust has allowed me to share the exact steps we've worked through to improve their credit. Now the I can pass on the knowledge to others.

Table of Contents

INTRODUCTION

When I found out I was pregnant, it felt like an initiation.

On some level, I knew that nothing would ever be the same. I moved from the state of being a single woman, responsible for no one other than myself, to the state of being someone's mother.

I was converted.

I thought deeply about what mental, financial, and emotional gifts my mother left for me and how deeply she impacted and still impacts my life.

In those reflections, I realized that I had the sacred opportunity of directly impacting my daughters mental, spiritual and financial future.

Had this responsibility been placed on me seven years ago I wouldn't be ready.

There was a time when I was broke, in debt, and had no idea what credit was or how it would ultimately impact my life. Just as many of you reading this book, your first brush with credit did not occur until you were disqualified for a loan, a car, or something else you needed to use credit to attain. The first time I ever learned about credit, I was about 20 years old and I tried to buy a car. I was denied.

In addition to the denials, I needed a financial overhaul. When I had a bank account, I constantly had overdraft fees. When I couldn't get a bank account, I remember having to use a RushCard in order to get my direct deposit for work. There was a $1.00 fee for every transaction that was made. Essentially, the RushCard charged me to use their card and have access to my money. In order to make ends meet, I would get cash advances, which pretty much cost me $50 to borrow $500. Credit cards, maxed. In every way, shape, and form, I had a poverty mindset. I was always in a position that made me rob Peter to pay Paul. There was almost always more month than money.

There were a series of events that led me to get my act together, but long story short, I was tired. I was tired of not having the freedom to have the options money afforded me. I was tired of being stressed about money. I was tired of being told no when I applied for something. I was tired of existing in a space that didn't fully represent who I believed myself to be. Most importantly, as a Christian woman, I couldn't wrap my head around the idea that this is the life God could have possibly wanted for me. Something had to change.

Looking back, I realized that if I didn't get my act together, that would've been the financial blueprint I would've given my daughter. I can proudly say that my daughter does not have to worry about money or poverty because I converted my credit and mindset around money.

Converting is the act of moving from one state to another. That would be the same as moving from being single to being a mother. For my mother that meant moving from being married, to raising three children alone, and bearing all of the financial burden.

For you, after you read this book, you can move from the state of passing on debt to leaving a financial legacy, from a poverty mindset to a wealth mindset, and from financial trauma to financial freedom.

Credit is not sexy topic. Credit is not a topic people venture to talk about, let alone write an entire book about. Being that credit is the second largest market in the world, it's fair to say that it matters. With the current state of the economy (this is being written during the COVID-19 pandemic), one could argue that credit and money will matter now more than ever.

Having good credit saves you hundreds of thousands of dollars over the course of your life and your credit score can be used as an asset to make you money.

I want you to imagine for a second having the access good credit affords you. Getting credit card companies to pay you to use their cards, learning what your money can do for you, and having the bonus of passing on these skills to your children.

Now that this image is crystalized in your mind, I want you to understand a few key elements to this book that will help you get closer to your credit score conversion.

This is not another traditional "self-help" book. EVERYTHING you will read and encounter is information I have curated, calculated, applied, and systemized for over seven years.

This book was written for you to educate yourself on the inner workings of credit. Once you have finished reading this book and have begun putting the suggested steps in motion, you should be better equipped to fix your credit yourself and not have to spend upwards of $5K trying to pay someone to do it for you. I also want to save you a lot of time and effort that can be eaten up by doing the wrong things the wrong way. As a consumer credit expert, I will tell you firsthand that credit repair can be pricey. If you want someone to do it for you, that is okay, but you can do it alone if you have the determination and tools to get it done. This book is THE tool. The contents of this book has undoubtably helped thousands of individuals join the elite class of people who possess the power to make informed credit decisions and have access to all the luxuries leveraging credit affords.

If you follow these steps, you will be arming yourself with the information you need to change the course of your credit score. Anything I have learned, you will learn. There is nothing being withheld from you. All of my "secrets" are laid out for you in this book. All you have to do in exchange is read the book and apply the principles to the best of your ability. Also, I want you to know that you will be able to double check everything written here for yourself. The only purpose for this book is to consolidate this information in a meaningful way that works.

Who Can Benefit Most From This Book?

To the mother that didn't learn the basics about money and credit or didn't major in finance, this book is for you. If you are a mother looking to pass down a great resource that your kids can use to get a head start, this book is for you. If you're older and your kids are older, and you want to fix some of the mistakes you made in your heyday, this is book is still for you. It's never too late to lead by example.

There is something here for mothers at every stage of their journey to get started toward learning about and fixing their credit.

The Strategy

The book is strategically structured in a way that forces the information to build upon itself. That means you have to read the book from chapter to chapter. Do not skip ahead. Yes, primitive, I know. In today's day and age, it seems as if everyone wants the microwave answer to complex problems. I had to fight the urge to structure the book that way. The book is intentionally designed so that you pay the price of reading it. There are no shortcuts. *When people pay a price, they pay attention.* The price is not how much the book cost. The price I'm referring to is the time you will have to spend actually learning the information if you want to get real expert results. You will get the most out of this information if you follow how the book is intentionally outlined. You have to read the book. You'll thank me later.

Section One

This section is dedicated to educating you. It's the shortest section. I won't be lecturing you, but there are some key pieces of information that will fall into place very nicely when it comes to creating your credit strategy, negotiating with creditors, or when you're sending out your dispute letters.

Section Two

Section Two contains the meat and potatoes. In this section, you will get to apply the information in Section One and actually start repairing your credit. You will receive detailed insights into what to put in your dispute letters to set the bureaus straight, credit strategy to trip up collection agencies, and score hacks the average consumers don't know about.

Section Three

This section is dedicated to rebuilding. If you've successfully completed Sections One and Two, Section Three will show you how to get your score increased. It has a ton of resources to add positive credit history to your report and addresses key issues that you will need to deal with so that you don't go back to poor credit.

Section Four

So, after you educate, repair, and rebuild, then what? You maintain. In my opinion this section is the most important. Credit repair is easy. Maintaining credit is hard. I say that because there are steps you have to take regularly to ensure that you are not compromising your credit and that it's available when you need it.

To make things even easier for you, I was sure to keep things super simple, well defined, and well structured. I hope you're prepared to start taking these small, but impactful steps to your new score.

Now without further ado, let's convert some credit scores.

CHAPTER 1

Straight To The Points

"Isn't it sad that we have to gain control of the artificial numbers placed upon us by others to regain some control of our lives?"
– Rick Gregory

I could never fully wrap my head around why credit was needed. Like, who decided that these three numbers, dished out by three major companies, would decide my financial fate forever? With my credit report opened in front of me and a face full of confusion, I realized that I didn't understand why credit mattered so much. Up to that point, all I had seen around me was the negative impact of not having good credit and if the consequences were anything like the process of fixing my credit, I wanted out.

So, why? Why does any of this even matter?

For starters, I don't know if anyone else is like this, but if I don't understand "why" I am doing something, it makes it challenging for me to commit to seeing it through.

It became blatantly clear to me that credit mattered because of the access that it offered financially.

Many people in the personal finance space argue that cash is king. My mother, a working woman, had some cash but it only took us so far. As a matter of fact, I would argue that cash made things harder in raising us in many ways. When credit was needed, we would either have to do without or we would have to be subjected to much higher interest rates. So instead of having more money to take care of her kids, she ended up in a situation where money was being spent to pay down interest. The system is truly backwards.

Credit also slips its way into so many aspects of our lives. Here are a few ways credit impacts us almost daily.

Relationships

There is some weird statistic floating around that states 50% of marriages end in divorce. I don't know if it's really 50%, but I will tell you I have seen how differences in managing money and poor credit can put a strain on many relationships. In my years of credit repair, there are many couples that have come to see me to meet their goal of buying a home, refinancing, and/or starting a business, but they had a hard time simply because they couldn't see eye to eye. As a child, I saw this idea played out in my parents' marriage before my father left. Now as an adult with a small child of my own, I can understand how money and credit can put a huge strain on a relationship.

If you ever consider going back into the dating world, consider this: Love is important but so is financial longevity. If your partner has a poor score, your financial future will be negatively impacted. The same can be said for you – your poor score and debt can hurt someone else's ability to move forward financially. The phrase "for richer and for poorer" is not put in traditional wedding vows to be cute. Establishing a good credit foundation is a great way to begin the plan to avoid the "for poorer" possibility. Get ready by knowing your partner's score early on and how much debt you will be dealing with. Think about it. Here is why you should know what your partner's relationship to money is: If a lender wouldn't get into a lending agreement with them, should you? Just a few questions to think about.

THIS IS IMPORTANT: If you are entering into a long term committed relationship, I would even dare to argue that not looking into your partner's finances is irresponsible.

Let me bring this home for you. Let's say that you are newly married and ready to buy a home. When buying a home, there are a few financial factors that will be considered before a lender will approve a home loan. One of the factors that the lender will consider is the lower of the two credit scores. Sad, but true.

So, you say to yourself, "I'll just let my partner buy the house in their name alone." That would be ideal; however, removing your partner from the mortgage application may backfire. Even if the loan is approved, it may not be approved for as much as it would have if there were two people on the loan application. The income of one individual simply may not be enough to support the purchase of the home.

This is not just going to be your life partner; this is going to be your money partner too. It's just something to consider before jumping the broom.

Home Buying

Let's stay with the example of home buying. Buying a house is going to be one of the biggest life purchases you will ever make, but it is extremely rewarding. Your kids will have a safe stable home to live in, you are gaining an asset that builds equity, and you can pass it on to your children after you transition from life to death. All these benefits come at a cost and can be even more costly if you have bad credit.

Story Time

Nathalie (Hi, that's me) wants to buy a house for $350K. Nathalie has to take out a loan because she does not have the cash up front to buy a house. Nathalie goes to a lender to get pre-approved for a mortgage because she has great credit, a low debt-to-income ratio, and the income to support the purchase. The bank gives her the loan at a low interest rate. For the sake of this example, let's say the bank gives Nathalie an interest rate of 4%. If Nathalie agrees to pay this mortgage over thirty years on a house worth $350K, she will be paying roughly $1,671 a month for her mortgage. Furthermore, the entire cost of her home (including interest) will be $601,543. Of the total cost of the home, you would have paid $251,543 in interest (at the 4% interest rate).

Now let's flip this scenario to Nathalie's evil sister Natasha.

Natasha wants to buy the same house Nathalie was looking into purchasing (because she is evil) valued at $350K. Natasha has to take out a loan because she does not have the cash up front to do so. Natasha goes to a broker to get pre-approved for a mortgage and because she has poor credit, they give her the loan at a higher interest rate. For the sake of this example let's say they give Natasha an interest rate of 20%. If Natasha agrees to pay this mortgage over thirty years, she will be paying roughly $5,848 month for her mortgage. Furthermore, the entire cost of her home (including interest) will be $2,105,483.

Of the total cost of the home, she would have paid $1,755,483 in interest on a home that was initially valued at $350,000.

Now this is an *extremely* simplified and *extremely* exaggerated example of what goes into home buying, but both examples demonstrate how credit can influence the home buying process.

The same goes for other large purchases, such as a car. The lower your score, the higher your rates. To make matters worse, your car insurance can also be impacted by your credit score. With the exceptions of some states, many car insurance companies will check your credit score to determine the probability of you filing a claim in the future. Using predictive analytics tools and the same comparative mathematical algorithm as the credit bureaus, insurance companies use information on your credit report to determine what your premiums could be and even if you're a high-risk driver. So, in addition to needing good credit to buy a car, you will need good credit to insure that car and get a great rate.

Paying Interest

While we are on the topic of interest, whenever I speak or do workshops, I like to emphasis this point:

Interest is not in your interest

Interest is not in your interest

Interest is not in your interest

Read it again and again.

Interest is not for you. It is the bank's way of making money. The amount of money you pay in interest is directly related to your credit score. Let me tell you how backwards the credit system is. You have to build credit to gain access to life's luxuries, but if you use credit, you have to do so at a cost. Furthermore, the lenders and creditors use your score to determine your interest rate, and the higher your credit, the lower the interest rate. But if you have poor credit, you pay more in interest. Backwards. When we get to really understand what credit is at its core, you'll see why the system is created this way and why we will never, ever pay interest on a credit card. As a matter of fact, I am going to show you how I get my credit card companies to pay me every month!

Finding a Job

My mother went to nursing school to create a better life for us. She was one of those women who believed strongly in education as a way of improving her circumstances. It worked out for her that she was able to graduate from school and enter the workforce. Imagine if after all those years of studying and fighting for her degree she was denied work because of her credit. How would she have provided for her children?

Believe it or not, some employers, especially in the corporate or executive positions, look at your credit to determine if you are a viable candidate or not. If you are looking for a high-paying and prestigious job, your credit will matter.

Employers may look at your credit report and score to determine if you are financially responsible.

Employers get a watered-down version of your report, but employers or potential employers can look to see whether or not you're a high-risk candidate. An example would be a company that issues a company card. Some companies use this practice of pulling reports to be sure that they remove the possibility of stealing or misappropriation of money. If you have demonstrated poor financial management in the past, the company you are applying to can view you as a liability and not an asset. Not so equal opportunity if you ask me, but that's not the point. Just ONE more reason to have good credit.

Owning a Business

Let's say the previous lesson does not apply to you because you have a goal of one day owning your own business. Your personal credit rating may come into question when you're trying to gain funding, build business credit, or manage your businesses finances.

When you first start a business, there are several options to finance a business, but if you choose to go the lending route, you will need to use your personal credit as backing for the company loan or line of credit. This is called being a personal guarantor. When your business is new, you may not have enough cash coming into the business to support the life of a loan, so lenders will use your personal credit to support your ability to repay and ensure you are incentivized to get their money back to them.

You do not have to get lending to run a business and many people have started businesses debt free. Others choose to take on a loan because they may not have all of the capital they need upfront to grow a business as far or as fast as they want to.

Helping Your Children

Over the years, I have had the privilege of working on my mother's credit, my credit, my sister's credit, and for a number of family members. Once we got our financial affairs in order, we each leveraged our credit to help one another.

After we improved our credit, I realized one important lesson. Wealth is built through the family unit. As a single mother, my mother would've had a very challenging time trying to build wealth alone. Couple that with the fact that she could not pass on what she didn't know. The same was true for my cousins and close friends. A lot of us, the children of immigrants, had to or still have to figure it out.

Now that I have a daughter, my biggest blessing is to be able to pass on the blueprint for financial freedom for her. You can do the same for your children too, but that would mean dedicating yourself to improving your credit so they can leverage your credit when they are of age. Study this book, learn it inside out so that you can do right by your children later on and pass on these lessons.

Good credit starts with you.

If your kids have not established credit yet and they need guardians to assist with co-signing, you will want to be able to do so. Also, as a parent, you know kids learn as you **do** long before they do as you **say**. Think of the money blueprint, habits, and legacy you are leaving behind. The dodged collection calls? They see that. The statements you make about money? They internalize that. If not for you, learn for them – give them an advantage in the world.

Having a Bank Account

In addition to credit, you will need access to cash. I know many of us are still at the age where we remember our maternal figures hiding money under the mattress, but those days are over. It didn't seem obvious to me how credit and bank accounts were tied at first, but upon getting my first credit card, I slowly realized why it is very difficult to have one without the other. In order to make the payments on your credit card monthly, the money to make a payment will have to come out of your bank account. Now with the rise in trying to improve credit worthiness for consumers, programs like Experian Boost (more on how to use this strategically later) are allowing you to upload banking information to improve your score.

Life's Luxuries

A lot of life's little luxuries rely heavily on the credit system. Many companies like utility companies are running credit checks to determine if you should be paying a deposit/ down payment or not on things like cell phones, electricity, or heating/cooling services.

When you look at the entire picture, you have to understand how the system works so you can beat it. Beating the interest trap is a way to ensure that you do not burn hundreds and thousands of dollars over your lifetime – because this is for life. Bad credit is costly. All that money you will be saving in interest can go toward providing, protecting, and preparing your children for their future.

Also, consider the fact that if you ever did decide to date again, you would be a financial asset to your partner. Lastly, but most importantly, having good credit and getting your finances in order is going to relieve the financial anxiety you go through every month trying to rob Peter to pay Paul. Once we get through this book, those days are over. You can get close to the life you deserve for you and your family.

In the next chapter, we will look at what credit really is, and it's not what you expect.

CHAPTER 2

The Keys To Unlimited Credit Access

This chapter couldn't be left out of the book. This is an important topic that we need to get out of the way as soon as possible. Once you really understand it, your perspective will shift on what it is and how to play the game to win.

So what the heck is credit anyway? Where did it come from?

We already explored why it matters, but let's talk about what it is and why the system was designed. It's not what you think. I promise.

Sometime around 1529, the word credit came into our lexicon with roots in French, Latin, and Italian. The essence and meaning of the word credit is the same in all the languages – "trust."

Credit is trust. It is an quantifiable honor system used to build trust between people, their businesses, and the banks that extend the credit.

Let's say you were loaned ten dollars. If this is your first time borrowing, there is no way to honestly know if the lender will get their money back. For the risk, the lender has to take for the trouble of having their money away from them for some time, they are going to charge you an additional 10% of the original amount loaned. The one dollar paid in interest is agreed upon. So, you do whatever you initially need to do with the money and now it's time to pay it back.

Depending on the terms we set, you agree to pay the money back in ten payments over ten weeks and the interest is also calculated and paid, since you're making the payments with the trust that the lender will receive their money in full.

The ability for you to borrow money in the future will depend on the following things:

Trust and Risk

These are some things to consider. Let's say that you didn't pay on time. Should the lender take that risk again? If trust was broken, the lender wouldn't be able to feel a hundred percent comfortable, so they may hike up the interest rate to make it worth their while, just in case you take a long time to pay or for the risk you may not pay at all.

The same could be said if you paid according to the terms and there wasn't an issue with repayment. The lender would be more willing to give you whatever and however much you wanted and may actually lower the interest rate because they have such a good rapport with you or because trust was established.

So, in essence, credit is a way to measure risk based on previously established or perceived trust. In order to determine whether someone is trustworthy or not, there was an algorithm built to calculate the relationship between risk and trust. This algorithm is called FICO – short for Fair Issac and Company. This algorithm was named after the two men that created the system. The FICO score uses an algorithm to determine the risk of lending to you by how heavy the "trust" scale tips (more trust, less risk; less trust, more risk). Your score is the measure of trust and your interest rates are the risk lenders believe they are taking when they lend to you. If you look at credit through this filter, it will clear up a lot of confusion.

Credit is your money borrowing fingerprint. The same way your actual fingerprint is unique to you, credit pretty much works the same way. Credit reports are mostly meant to reflect how you have been managing your relationship to trust over time and the trust that has been established between the borrower and the lender. This is super important to know because as we dive into later chapters about how to leverage your credit, you'll need to familiarize yourself with the blueprint to understand how to build your credit "trust" in the most effective way.

It may not be the best feeling in the world to hear this narrative because for many of us, we may see ourselves as trustworthy. In many cases most people are. Many individuals that would be higher risk, fell on hard times and their current standing in life is not necessarily due to irresponsibility or lack of trust. If you had a medical concern, those bills can add up quickly. If you were part of the 2008 mortgage crisis, at the time, that foreclosure could have greatly affected you as it did hundreds of thousands of Americans. Recently divorced? Yeah, the change in income, splitting expenses and all of the other financial factors that you must consider in divorce can contribute to you becoming a higher risk. For many of you reading the book, you may be torn between credit and making sure that your children are taken care of. Many creditors and lenders have hardship programs for that reason – they understand that life happens. Unfortunately, the algorithm isn't smart enough to detect hardship, only what's reported to it.

Feelings about trust aside, when you borrow money, lenders are always going to measure their risk. They have to. That is the cost of doing business and lending money. Are you high risk? Or are you a low risk?

That's what they want to know and your score is going to reveal this to them. In addition to your score, creditors/lenders (I will use them interchangeably) use a number of factors to determine how much of a risk you will be to them. In the future, one thing to consider before you go to acquire any new credit, is to ask the lenders what other factors they are using to determine whether you are a potential high-risk or low-risk consumer. Each lender has a list of criteria they use to get you approved. Once we go over how to read your report, you will be able to know how likely you are to get approved or what needs to be addressed in your report to also increase your chances based on the perceived risk to lenders.

Remember: We will be looking at credit through the eyes of the lender. Your credit score is one of the primary elements that allows creditors to determine the risk they will take in lending money to you. If you learn how to diminish those risks, the rewards will be great for you!

Access

Another uncommon and unpopular idea about what credit is, is the idea that credit is about access.

Credit is simply what's available to you. Many people get scared of the word credit because they believe that credit is a portal to debt. Again, credit is just what you have available to you over and over again based on trust. Debt is what you use and owe.

Your ability to create a distinction in your mind is key to *managing* credit. When you make a credit purchase, you are essentially taking what it cost today and spreading the cost over time with interest. For example, if you buy a home, you are buying the home at its current value and spreading the cost of the home over a 15- or 30-year term. The amount you owe until the balance is zero is debt. Whether it's good debt or bad debt isn't the argument here. Stay focused. It is debt nonetheless, because it is owed, and it was not purchased in cash outright.

Essentially, when you are loaned any money, you are going to be paying more over time because you didn't have the money to pay it up front. I use this example with big purchases like a home. Most people don't have $100K-to-$300K up front to pay for a home. Depending on who your lender is, they will look at your score, determine how high of a risk you are, and lend you the money at an interest rate that will make the house cost more over time because you had to borrow the money. The interest is their incentive for lending the money to you upfront. There are ways around interest – especially with credit cards. As I stated earlier, debt is what you owe, and credit is the amount of access you have to debt. At the end of the book, I am going to outline expert level tricks to beat interest and how to get credit card companies to pay you.

Now that we've cleared up what credit really is, please know that credit isn't anything to be afraid of. Again, technically, if you never fully use your access to credit, you can't be in debt, but if you know how to make credit bend to your will, you can leverage all that credit has to offer without owing massive amounts of money. I know some people may be a little leery, so let's be clear: mismanaged credit cards or money can lead to credit card debt and bad credit. I'm not eliminating that possibility. This is what credit is and principally, what it isn't.

RECAP:

- Credit is not new. This system has been around for a very long time, and it must work to some degree for it to have been around so long. Yes, there are broken structural pieces, but if you learn how to make credit work for you, you get to leverage it just as others have for hundreds of years.

- Credit is a system built on trust and the FICO score is an algorithm that measures a lender's ability to trust you with respect to the level of risk you pose to them as a borrower.

- Credit is also just the amount of access you have. If you access too much credit, you can fall into debt if it's mismanaged and there is no plan in place to repay, but the two are not the same.

- We are going to learn to look at our credit as lenders do so we can maximize our credit over time.

In the next chapter we will look at all of the elements that make up your score. The goal is to get intimate with these factors because they will follow you through every step of the repair, they will inform your decision making moving forward, and they will help you pick which resources from the resource section will work best to boost your score and drive the algorithm to raise your score.

CHAPTER 3

The Down Low On FICO

A s we went over in the previous chapter, credit is in part an assessment of risk. The risk is measured by an algorithm and that is how your score is generated. When we understand all of the working parts that the algorithm tests for, we can manipulate each element point by point – literally.

To begin, please know that the best and most accurate algorithm or scoring model is the FICO score. It is also the score most widely accepted by lenders, so this is the ONLY model we will be using throughout the book.

The typical FICO score ranges from 300 to 850 and is calculated based on these five main factors:

1. Payment History

2. Debt Usage

3. Length Of History

4. Account Mix

5. Hard Inquiries

Each of these factors make up an exact percentage of your score that, when added up, will amount to 850 exactly.

1. Payment History- 35% of your score

2. Debt Usage- 30% of your score

3. Length of History- 15% of your score

4. Account Mix- 10% of your score

5. Hard Inquiries 10% of your score

We're about to get into some basic math, but it's for your own good. I promise.

If you have an 850 credit score, payment history can account for a total of 297.5 points. Late or unpaid payments can potentially drop your score between 30-100 points. This would depend on how long the creditor goes unpaid and how recent the account has been delinquent.

If you do the math for each credit score factor and corresponding percentage, as promised it will add up to a total of 850 points.

Score Factor	Impact	Total Contributing Points
Payment History	35%	297.5
Debt Usage	30%	255
Length of History	15%	127.5
Account Mix	10%	85

Hard Inquires	10%	85
Total	100%	850 Points

As you can see, all five areas contribute in order to get that "perfect" score. Let's examine each factor and exactly what you need to know about how each contributes to your score.

Payment History

The name speaks for itself. It is the number one factor that determines your score as far as possible points lost is concerned. Creditors use this information to determine if you make your payments, if you make those payments on time, if you missed payments, and for how long you missed payments. This accounts for 35% (297.5 points) of your score.

PRO TIP: PAY ON TIME AND PAY WHAT YOU AGREED TO PAY

That's the big takeaway here. It's important.

Debt Usage

Debt usage is the second most important factor that can possibly impact your score. Debt usage is essentially *HOW* you are using the money (or credit) you have access to. As it pertains to debt usage, unfortunately I have not found a perfect ratio; but any time debt usage was over 30% it would have had a negative impact on a credit score. Also, the general rule of thumb is to keep your debt usage between 10%-29%. I wouldn't even risk touching the 1% they claim you can access before your score is impacted.

That means if you start off with a card that has a $300 credit limit, you probably don't want to use more than $29 at a time within the same billing cycle. When credit bureaus examined the score of those that have an 800 score or more, they found that their debt usage was only 1% of their total credit limit. A little tidbit you may want to hold on to.

Length of History

Herein lies reason number three as to why you need to think in terms of the "long" game and not try to take short cuts. In the "length of history" section of your credit report, creditors will be looking at how long of a credit history you have established and how you have been managing your credit over time.

Every year an account gets older (and remains in good standing) you get a few points. You are basically being rewarded for keeping up your end of the bargain by agreeing to the terms set between you and the creditors.

The takeaway from this section is that you need to have some kind of credit over time because creditors use this information to determine what kind of borrower you will be in the future. This will help them determine if they want to play the long game with you.

Account Mix

Account mix makes up 10% of your score. It may not seem significant (10% or 85 points), but when you're trying to get a score increase or maintain your score, every point counts.

Account mix refers to the types of credit accounts you have. There are two kinds:

Revolving debt

Installment debt

The installment debt usually comes in the form of a large sum that is broken down into smaller payments (with interest) and you agree to pay equal parts of the large sum until it is paid off. An example of an installment debt is a car/auto loan. The agreed amount paid monthly is an installment payment.

Revolving debt has more flexible payments; you borrow and pay back to maintain a balance. It's also referred to as revolving because you can revolve the amount used and amount owed. An example of this may be a credit card. It's true that credit cards also have an amount that is expected to be paid, but this can change due to a number of factors.

Lenders use this information to know whether or not you can manage different types of debt. By looking at this information, lenders believe they are getting a well-rounded view of how you manage different types of credit.

With this knowledge, it is not intended that you run out and get a bunch of different types of loans/credit cards to vary your credit profile. The goal here is to be equipped with knowledge to make informed decisions. When you speak to a lender (assuming you will have to again sometime in the future) you should be asking what type of loan it is so you know how it will potentially affect your score. If you have a decent score and you can't seem to get it to increase for some reason, this may be a factor. The more you know, the better prepared you will be to ask the right questions.

NOTE: Personal loans (installment debt) are rather difficult to come by. I will be providing a resource that allows you to get an account that shows up on your credit as an installment loan, has instant approvals, and is also way to save money.

Hard Inquiries

Have you ever walked into Macy's and they asked you if you wanted to apply for a Macy's card? If you decide to apply for one, Macy's (or whoever manages their credit accounts) will gather your credit record and decide if they want to issue you that card or not. The process of peeking into your credit history with the intention of extending credit is called an Inquiry. If your credit is great, you will be issued a card and approved for a line of credit with Macy's. If your credit is bad, you can anticipate getting denied.

The reason credit inquiries affect your score is because the more you inquire about acquiring new debt, the greater the risk you are to a lender. Think about it like this, if you were asking me to borrow $10.00 and there was a way for me to see that you've asked 20 other people for ten dollars, it would concern me.

1. If you have too much you need to pay back, how do I know you will pay me back?

2. What is your current situation that you have to ask so many people for money in such a short period of time?

This is kind of how the creditors look at it. This is why they want to know how many times you ask. The more you ask for debt, the deeper it affects your credit score. Although inquires only account for roughly 85 points, they add up and they add up quickly. The credit bureaus know that at some point lenders will have to inquire about your credit, so they throw you a couple freebies (anything over four inquiries in a two-year period and you start to see your score go down). Luckily, after two years they fall off and you can inquire again without a reduction in points. Remember every point counts.

Now that you know what makes up your score, let's look at how it's all being reported. In order to do that you will need to pull your credit report. I want to set some expectations before you look at your report as it can be a bit intimidating, but this is a major turning point for most people. If you can make it through that chapter, your odds of success increase exponentially. It's only fair that you were warned, and the following chapter will help set up the mindset needed to approach your report. Knowing how to read your report will help you spot exactly what is hurting your score. If you don't know what's hurting your score, how can you fix what you have not confronted?

With that being said, let's dive into the next chapter.

CHAPTER 4

Preparing For The Dispute Process

E ven though this book is meant to help you streamline your credit repair journey, there may be a few bumps in the road that will require a certain mindset and a certain level of resilience to go through. There is also a clear link between finances and stress, so let's set those expectations now. Those who develop the mindset needed to deal with the demands of credit repair will win and continue to see those wins long after the repair is over. Let me tell you how to set your expectations and emotions up to win.

Patience

The repair process takes time and lots of it. From the time you send a letter to the bureaus, by law, they have 30 days to get back to you from the time they receive it. Even then, they have various stall tactics (which I will show you how to beat) that buy them time and prolong the process even more. I also need you to know that the bureaus are private institutions. It is at the bureau's discretion that items are removed. Many people give up for that reason alone. The logic is why should you try if they are the final deciding factor? Well, even though the bureaus are the deciders, in order for them not to abuse the power, there are governing bodies that ensure they are operating ethically.

More on this later. Please be patient through the process. Almost everything can be figured out – which brings me to my next point.

Solution Oriented

Again, everything can be figured out. For every problem there is a solution. You may not see the solution just yet, but there is almost always one. This is what you have to keep in mind. There will always be a problem. Always. What sets most successful people apart is where they choose to place their energy. If you place all your energy looking at the problems, you'll always find them.

If you spend the energy seeking solutions, you'll be surprised at how creative your mind gets at finding solutions. Most of us aren't programmed to strive towards the solutions. Being solution-oriented is a muscle that you will need to develop through this process. One way to start is by asking questions. Don't be afraid to ask when you need information or you're not sure. Someone has the answer you need.

Self-forgiveness

To piggyback from my previous point about asking, some people are afraid to ask because they are ashamed. The shame could come from being in the position to ask in the first place or just being ashamed that you don't have the answers. Who cares! ASK! Some people want to sit on their high horse and not share information, but that's fine, move on to the next person that is willing to sit with you patiently and compassionately. These people exist.

Also, I need you to forgive yourself. Extend yourself some grace. For many of you, this is the first time you are looking at your credit report and it can be overwhelming. Take the time you need to grieve what your credit is right now, but I also ask you to please celebrate the fact that by reading this book and taking the step that you need to be where you want to be. Soon you will be celebrating! Forgive yourself. You are on the path to financial self-improvement.

My last point is to remember that you are not your credit score. Even though those numbers have major implications on your life, they are just numbers. They go up and down depending on what you do, but they are not you. Outside of the score you are a woman, a mother, and a whole person.

Depersonalize yourself from the score and the numbers, so you can take a rational and practical approach to repairing your credit. I need you to think of the numbers that you first see when you pull up your report as a baseline. This is the starting point. That's it. Hope that helps.

Change Your Relationship To Money

Many of us were not taught about money, so there may be a lot to unpack. Some of these programmed ideas about money, spending, lending, and borrowing will come up during this journey. For some, money is a mark of success. In seeing money as a mark of success, we may try to keep up with everyone else and overspend. In other cases, some people spend it to feel better about themselves or as a way to relieve stress. This mindless spending often doesn't account for what's coming in and what's going out of your wallet. If you're afraid of money, you may make some unsound decisions around it that only seem to prove your fears right later on. Fear also stops you from investing money in the right places. Then, the vicious cycle of credit card debt and lack of money continues. The repair journey will expose your relationship to money, the changes that need to be made, and where you are resistant to money. Examine how you feel at any given point, these emotions will be helpful or detrimental to the journey. It's your job to respond, so pay attention.

Organization

Staying organized is a way to help yourself not get overwhelmed through the process. If you're searching for papers, misplacing things, can't find your ID or Social Security card when you need it – it's going to make this process even more overwhelming and burn time. Remember, bureaus have 30 days to get back to you, so you need to stay on top of any correspondence that comes in. Stay on top of everything by creating a streamlined system that will keep you accountable and make this process a lot easier.

Invest In Yourself

When people pay, they pay attention. Period. Putting money into yourself and your credit goal is the number one way to ensure that you continue to pay attention to your credit long after it is repaired. The more time, effort, and money you pay, the less likely it will be for you to repeat the cycle that got you here in the first place. The amount of money you are going to spend repairing and rebuilding your credit is nothing compared to what you will pay for having poor credit. This is not the time to skimp or cut corners. Pay up and you're likely to get the results you need.

Reward Yourself

I don't want this to be an entirely taxing and negative experience for you. We as humans cannot function at our best when there is always tension or stress around a topic or a certain environment. I HIGHLY encourage you to reward yourself along the way. Find some inexpensive ways (that do not involve compromising your credit even more) that will allow you to keep motivated along this journey. Have something to look forward to by setting some goals and feeling the joy associated with meeting them. When accounts are deleted, celebrate. When your score goes up, celebrate. When you pay down a credit card, celebrate. Celebrate your accomplishments. You deserve it for the hard work you're about to put into your financial Future.

Face The Facts

Some of the emotional elements of this journey may be deeper than just needing your credit fixed. This is the moment that having a real intimate conversation with yourself is important. If you are overspending and you need help in that way, it would be best if you seek help from an organization that can attend to those needs. If you find yourself in debt due to gambling, there are also organizations that can help you for free to address the deeper emotional issues that are tied to your money.

It's only right to be very fair and balanced in saying that maybe you can come back to this book at another time. Addressing your relationship to money is important and should be done first. The book will be here when you're ready.

A lot of information was just covered. In the next few chapters, you're going to encounter even more information, but as promised it will build on the last thing you read. In the next chapter, you'll have the chance to get real intimate with your credit report. This information will allow you to repair your credit now, but it will also allow you to identify what may cause any score changes you see in the future.

The report is exactly what lenders see before they decide to lend you money. The report also contains all of the moving parts that make up your credit. When one element is off balance, the entire score suffers. This is another reason why reading your report, understanding your report, and how it contributes to the make-up of your score is really important. Now, let's go over how to read your report, get into disputing negative items, learning what your rights are as a consumer, and a whole lot more that will allow your credit to become squeaky clean. If you made it this far, don't give up now.

CHAPTER 5

The Devil Is In The Details

Okay, so now we have a better understanding of what factors will affect your score, reasons why credit is important, and what you can expect through the process. Now let's get to reading your report, repairing and seeing how to make your score work for you.

No two credit reports are created the same. One of the differences you will see depends on what scoring model you are looking at. As mentioned earlier, there are different scoring models. Of all of the models the FICO model is the one that's been in existence the longest and is the most accurate (in my professional opinion). When you are reading your report, you want to use a monitoring service that shows you your FICO score. This automatically eliminates the option of using the likes of "Credit Karma." Nothing is wrong with Credit Karma, per se, but it only shows two of the three bureau reports and it doesn't always have all of the information listed. People like it because it is free and it updates regularly, but when it comes to credit monitoring with the goal of trying to get your credit repaired, a paid service with the most up-to-date and accurate information is what you need.

If you're looking for a good monitoring service with the most accurate reporting and reports that give you insights from all three bureaus, why not go to the source? Myfico.com is FICO's credit monitoring service that allows you to see the most up-to-date and accurate information with the most precise and up to-date scoring model. In addition to credit monitoring, they also offer your mortgage score, auto loan score, $1 million in identity theft insurance, and identity guard monitoring. All of these features come with the premier subscription they have, but you can still get the most accurate information about your report and score if you decide to go with a more cost-effective subscription plan. Either way, make sure you are picking the plan that shows you all three reports.

For the sake of demonstrating how to read your report, I will be using MyFico (MF) as my point of reference. If you want to follow along using MF, you'll get a better grasp of some of the things mentioned in this book. If not, don't worry, a lot of the same information being covered should be on any report you use. If you want to go with a different monitoring software, just be sure to double and triple check for accuracy.

Where Does The Information On Your Credit Report Come From?

This is a question that's important when it comes to understanding your report. The accounts, inquiries, late payments, or whatever you see has to come from somewhere. Experian, TransUnion, and Equifax (The Big 3) are private institutions. Each of these institutions agree to collect data about consumers (you) and keep it up-to-date for a fee. In exchange, other lenders can benefit by having the opportunity to peek (inquiry) at your information in order to make a lending decision when they are thinking of extending credit. Since the credit bureaus are private institutions that are getting paid to collect and maintain your data, you should know the following:

- There are laws that hold the bureaus to standards that ensure that they are practicing ethically and maintaining all fair reporting laws.

- Each account you see on your credit report pays each bureau to collect information about your relationship to them. This is why there may be variations between scores and accounts. It's a matter of which company wanted to pay to have your information stored with all or each of the three bureaus.

- Since information is being exchanged between so many people, companies, and hands it is not uncommon for there to be errors. It is your legal right to have those potential errors investigated and removed.

If you see one account on Experian, but not Equifax or TransUnion, the company reporting your credit history probably didn't want to pay all three bureaus. This entire practice of having a company pay to have your information stored, maintained, and updated with bureaus is called "Data Furnishing."

What Information Is Furnished?

When you open your MF dashboard online, look under Reports. There are a few things that you will notice, and they are broken up into categories.

Accounts

The accounts section is where all of your open and closed accounts will show up. There may be different types of accounts listed. For the most part, what you will see listed for each account is as follows:

- Payment history: For each account, the report also shows your payment history over a minimum of 24 months but could be longer in some instances. There will be a key at the top of your report that describes each payment history symbol and what it shows for your account. Green boxes marked "OK" show that your payment was made on time. If the payment wasn't made on time, it will show 30, 60, 90, or 120 days late.

- When you opened the account

- The kind of credit (installment, such as a mortgage or car loan, or revolving)

- Terms on credit accounts: This is the number of payments you have scheduled with a creditor. Most commonly this applies to loan accounts. For example, an auto loan may have a repayment plan scheduled over 36 months and a home loan may have a repayment plan scheduled over 360 months – it is not uncommon to see those terms outlined on your credit report.

- Whether the account is in your name alone, with another person (joint, co-signer, etc.), or if you're an authorized user on the account listed

- Total amount of the loan, high credit limit, or highest balance on the card

- How much you still owe (if anything is owed)

- Fixed monthly payments or minimum monthly amount due

- Status of the account (open, inactive, closed, paid, charged off, etc.)

- How well you've paid the account

- When the account was last updated

- Reporting company (original creditor or collector if it's a collection)

- Contact information for reporting company (mailing address and phone number)

- Account number (usually partial, hidden for your security, and is more than enough for a dispute)

All of this information should be present when looking at the account in order for this account to be considered "completed." There are times where there are accounts that have categories that are listed as "other." You may have to do a little digging to find out exactly what this account is – especially if it is an account that is hurting your credit.

Note: There may be unclear remarks that you are not familiar with, but you should familiarize yourself with what your report says about your payment history. For example, a "Charge Off" means that the creditor you supposedly owed gave up on trying to collect. This is a poor remark on your credit report, and you will want to look out for those kinds of status remarks. You may also see payment codes that are numerical from 1-9 or you may see codes like R1 or I1. Depending on how well all of the information was expressed, there should be a key that accompanies the code that shows you what the code means as it relates to your payment history.

When looking at your report, you should also see a section that outlines if you have any collection accounts or not. In this section, all of the account information we mentioned earlier should still be present. The only variation in information may be the company name and company contact information. Collection accounts are accounts that are seriously past due/delinquent. These accounts have most likely been sold off to a collection company or handed off to an attorney to try to collect all or part of what was owed. If the original company holding your credit account sold your debt to another company (collection company), the information for the collection company the debt was sold to would be present. In some cases, the original creditors information is present and in other cases it isn't. Either way, company name and the new contact information for either the original creditor or the debt purchaser (collection company) should be present. This is important to know, and we will get back to that later.

If you see any collections account, make a note of the following:

- **Creditor Name**: The official name of the company that is currently attempting to collect the debt

- **Account Number**: An identifying number for your account with the collection agency. *This may or may not be the same as the account number on your original debt. You may have to ask for a reference number that the company is using for your account with them.*

- **Original Creditor**: The name of the original creditor where you first allegedly had your debt. This could be an account that is listed on your credit report (such as a credit card) or an account that is not listed on your report (such as a library, video rental or cell phone company). If this creditor was a medical office, the name may be masked for your privacy.

- **Responsibility**: This indicates your responsibility for the account. For example, individual, joint, or co-signer

- **Condition**: The current status of your collection record. For example, open, closed, charged-off, or paid

- **Original Balance**: The amount of debt owed on the original account before it was transferred

- **Date Opened**: The date the account was transferred to the collection agency

- **Date Reported**: The date of the collection agency's last update to the bureaus

- **Remarks**: Notes about the account as reported to each credit reporting agency. For example, this section may note that the collector has been unable to locate you or that you have not yet paid the debt. If you are in the dispute process, there may also be notes/comments about the status of the dispute.

The next section is the part you want to be absolutely blank. The public records section is never a good story. If you have a public record on your credit report, you've had a problem that required litigation. It doesn't list arrests and criminal activities; just financial-related data, such as bankruptcies, judgments (money you may have been sued for) and tax liens. Those are the monsters that will destroy your credit faster than anything else.

NOTE: If you don't have any judgments, it's safe to skip over this section.

Here are definitions of the eight types of public records you could see listed on your credit report:

- **Bankruptcy**: A legal filing that relieves a person of responsibility for all or some of their debts because they are unable to pay

- **Tax Lien**: A claim filed by a local, state or federal tax agency against a person who owes back taxes

- **Legal Item**: A general filing. This is most commonly a judgment against you in a civil action.

- **Marital Item**: A legal filing related to a marital or divorce issue

- **Financial Counseling**: A public record indicating that a person has participated in financial counseling

- **Financial Statement**: A type of lien filed by a creditor against a person's property. This can be filed when a loan is secured against personal property (think collateral).

- **Foreclosure**: A record indicating that a mortgaged property has been taken over by the creditor because the borrower has defaulted on the loan

- **Garnishment**: A record indicating a court order to withhold some or all of a person's wages to repay a debt owed to a creditor

Within each public record, there will be a summary of information that is categorized according to the type of public record. If you are verifying the accuracy of any of the information listed, you will want to be sure they are all listed correctly. Here are some definitions of common record categories:

- **Type**: The type of record. For example, a tax lien, bankruptcy, garnishment, or judgment

- **Status**: Current status of the record. For example, released, filed, or dismissed

- **Date Filed/Reported**: Date when the record was initially filed or created

- **How Filed**: The role that you played in the public record. Usually the record is filed either individually or jointly

- **Reference Number**: Identifying number for the record

- **Released/Closing Date**: Date when the record was closed, released, or judgment was awarded

- **Court**: The court or legal agency that has jurisdiction over the record

- **Plaintiff**: The plaintiff in the case of a legal judgment

- **Amount**: Dollar amount of the lien or judgment

- **Remarks**: Notes regarding the public record as reported to the credit bureaus

- If the public record is a bankruptcy, three other fields will be visible depending on the chapter number (7,11,12, or 13).

- **Liability**: The amount the court found you to be legally responsible to repay

- **Exempt Amount**: The dollar amount claimed against you that the court has decided you are not legally responsible for

- **Asset Amount**: The dollar amount of total personal assets used in the court's decision. The Asset Amount can include items of value that can be used to pay debts

Inquiries

The final section you'll come across is the "Inquiries" section. An inquiry is a list of every company that's asked to see your credit report. Any time a company gets into the report, it will be posted to your credit report as an inquiry. That means if you try to apply for a credit card, it's listed as an inquiry. Have you been shopping for a car? Every time a dealership runs a credit report, it shows. If you call the credit bureau and ask for a copy of your report, you'll see a list of your inquiries. It's a very detailed entry record.

Inquiries are divided into two sections. "Hard" inquiries are inquiries you initiate by filling out a credit application. "Soft" inquiries are usually from a company or a group of companies that want to add you to a list of individuals who may be interested in promotional material/products. Soft inquiries lump you into a group of people who would be pre-qualified for what the company would have to offer and they may solicit you. Soft inquiries do not hit your credit report.

Note: Most inquiries are ignored by the FICO scoring models. The model has a buffer period that ignores inquiries within 30 days of getting a mortgage or a car loan. It also counts two or more "hard" inquiries in the same 14-day period as just one inquiry. You could have 30 in two weeks, and it only counts as one. This feature is worked into the algorithm to ensure people that are looking to rate shop do not feel the impact of the numerous inquiries it takes to get the best rate. If you're reading your report and you have been rate shopping, as long as it's in the allowed window, you don't have to worry about the potential damage to your credit score.

Having a lot of unrelated hard inquiries can be damaging. Potential creditors look at a large number of inquiries as a sign that you are trying to live your life on credit which means you might not have the means to pay back the debt. This is especially true if you've been applying for a lot of credit cards. Don't be fooled by the "pre-approval" offers. Pre-approvals usually come from those companies we mentioned earlier that did a soft inquiry to see if you would "pre-qualify" for a promotion they would like to offer you. Once you take the offer and put in an application, it is counted towards your report as a hard inquiry. Department stores are notorious for getting you to complete an application in exchange for a percentage off of your purchase whether you get approved for the card or not. If you don't get approved, there will still be a hard inquiry on your credit report that will take two years to come off. You're better off coupon hunting and not doing the damage to your credit score.

Note: Even if you have no plans on applying for new credit or you know you haven't in the last few years, you want to take a good look at the inquiries section because this is the first place you would see if you were a victim of identity theft. If you see a large number of inquiries on your credit report you did not approve, there is the possibility someone has gotten a hold of your information. This is a good time to take control and protect yourself from these thieves.

On your credit report, inquiries should also list the inquirers' information. The information will include the date the inquiry was made, the address, and phone number of the company that inquired into your credit. If this information is not present, you will want to write the bureaus to further investigate the nature of the inquiry.

Other Important Information

Every credit report, no matter where you source the report from, will have your personal information present. The personal information listed on your account includes:

- Name (Maiden or Married)

- Any names you've used in the past and variations of your name

- Date of birth

- Social Security number

- Current address and previous addresses

- Employment history (just the company names)

All of the information is meant to identify you. This is a section many people overlook, but please be sure this information is accurate and yours. Comb over the identifying information and be sure there aren't any addresses or places of employment that are not yours. If you have a popular name, this is especially important. You can't even begin to imagine how many times there have been credit reports with accounts that belong to another person with a similar name. If you are married and assume your partner's name, you don't know how many people may be floating around the U.S. with your new name. Be sure to check all of your identifying information. We will show you how to address this later in the repair section.

Reminder: All the information on your report is either being managed or furnished by human beings using machines. Humans are subject to error. Do your due diligence by making sure all of the information being reported is accurate.

What Information Isn't Furnished?

There are items you will not typically see on your credit report. Some people believe that their salary is located on their report, but that is simply not true. On loan or credit applications you may be asked about your finances so lenders can determine if you are able to repay, but it will not be reported to the credit bureaus.

Also, for all the right reasons, there is no information about your race, religion, nationality, gender, marital status, the political party you support, any crimes you've committed, or if you receive government assistance.

What If I Don't Want To Pay For Credit Monitoring?

Outside of paid credit monitoring being highly suggested during the repair process, you don't have to do it if you do not wish to. Some people just don't want to assume that expense and that is okay. Here are some alternate options.

Use free reporting sites

There are a number of reporting sites that will give you your credit information for free. They will show you most of the information that you need to know and update fairly regularly. The number one trusted site (supported by the government) is www.annualcreditreport.com. This is the only site that is approved by the government to issue you access to one free report per year from all three credit bureaus. If you choose to put your information into another site for a free annual report, you are putting yourself at risk of having your information stolen. One way to be sure you're dealing with a secured site (assuming you don't use annualcreditreport.com), is to check if the site is secured. Most secured sites have a padlock where the URL is which suggests the site is secured. Lastly, using annualcredireport.com happens to be the quickest way to access your report.

Contact Bureaus Directly

As mentioned, you are allowed one free report per year. Some people don't feel safe putting in their info online, so they choose to request their report directly from the bureaus. This option is good too. You just have to be diligent in sending the request and patient in getting a response (it could take up to six weeks to get your report). When we get to the repair portion of the book, I will show you exactly how to properly request your free report and there is even a template letter to help you do so.

Note: even if you choose to get a report online and pay for monitoring, request a report in writing to ensure the information they furnish to you

Experian & Equifax

Address:

Annual Credit Report Request Service

P.O. Box 105281

Atlanta, GA 30348-5281

Phone Number:

1-800-322-8228

TransUnion

Address:

TransUnion LLC

P.O. Box 1000

Chester, PA 19016

Phone Number:

1-800-888-4213

NOTE: TransUnion requests that their consumers to fill out a form. I suggest looking up the form online depending on when you're reading this – online information for the bureaus change regularly.

Denials

The less well-known method of obtaining your free copy of a credit report is when you are denied a loan, credit, housing application, or employment. If you are told that you've been denied for any of those reasons, get the denial in writing and send it to the credit bureaus with a request for an updated report. By law, the bureaus have to issue you a new report.

Disputes

After you ask the bureaus to investigate an item on your report, they will send you the most updated version of your credit report. You will usually see a face sheet showing what the result of your investigation/dispute was and then the remainder of the paperwork will be your most recent report. They will send this with every investigation request. This is a great way to access your report if you are working with limited funds or are cost sensitive.

Your Score

One of the key elements to your credit report is your score. That's why you're here right? It may be a good time to remind you that it is very difficult to get a "perfect score." Also, it may be a good time to note that these are three numbers that you will be addressing with the goal of improving.

As mentioned earlier, your FICO score can range from 300-850. Depending on where you fall in the range, creditors and lenders use this number as a metric for if you are a trustworthy person to lend to. They also use this information to take a look at the last two years of history with any given lender. Last, but definitely not least, they want to know what your rates and terms will be based on your credit score.

After you pull your report, the numbers you see are your baseline or starting point. It's important to know what lenders consider "good" or "great" credit so you have a bar to aim toward.

Score Ranges and Their Lending Meanings

- **Over 750** – you have excellent credit and will be able obtain credit easily

- **720 or more** – you still have very good credit and will be able to obtain credit easily

- **660 to 720** – this is an acceptable credit score. You can still get loans, but you may pay a higher interest rate

- **620 to 660** – creditors are going to be uncertain about lending you money

- **Less than 620** – you have poor credit history and will probably not be able to obtain credit on your own

More Reasons To Read Your Report

Identity Theft

Once a year may be too late if you are a victim of identity theft. Criminals love people who don't pay enough attention to their reports. A recent research study found that approximately 14 million people were victims of identity theft in 2018. Checking your report often allows you to know if there are any new items added to your report that may not be yours and gives you the option to take action quickly. In addition to checking more often, we recommend setting up alerts to your phone or email so you can get the updates as soon as the bureaus know. Again, criminals are hoping you don't look. They want to take advantage of your credit as long as you are not paying attention. Look and look often – this is the best way to protect your report.

Updates and Accuracies

Even if you have a new account that is indeed for you, checking your report often will allow you to ensure the account is being reported correctly. One of our clients from Vermont woke up one day to an alert that one of her lines of credit had been closed. She did not close the card at all. The closing of the card on her credit report impacted her score. Since we were able to address it immediately, she got all of her points back and the bureaus updated her account to reflect its accurate status – open. The most important takeaway here is that she was alerted and knew where and what to look for when she was looking at her report. Errors like this happen often. Checking your report puts you in the position to actively participate in keeping your information accurate and up to date.

Use Your Report To Establish A Baseline

When you look at your report, you will want to use this as the starting place for your repair. The information you see on your report on day one should look different by day sixty-one. As you move through the repair and rebuilding process, you will want to make sure you see the changes you are disputing and the new accounts you are adding. Your credit report will always be your reference point. This is where you will start, and this is where you will end. Get familiar with the information it contains with each step you take while improving your credit.

As we venture off to the next chapter, we are going to use the information on your report to map out your repair and plug in information from your reports to send off disputes to the credit bureaus. Let's get started on the most exciting part of the credit journey, watching those potentially harmful items get challenged and removed from your report.

CHAPTER 6

Rules Of The Repair

O kay, now for the part we've been waiting for – the repair.

The goal of the repair is to eliminate the items on our credit that could be hurting us. How that is done is through a series of letters you send to the bureau.

I have included letters in the "Appendix" section with letters that address the most common scenarios we run across in our firm.

Dispute Breakdown

We've already covered the step of going through the report and familiarized ourselves with what it consists of. The first step is to scan our reports again, but this time to see what items could be hurting us.

Common Negative Items

Late payments

Old inaccurate addresses

Incorrect name spelling

Charge offs

High balances

Bankruptcies

Public Records

Collection accounts

Too many inquiries

Wrong birth date/year

These are some of the most common items you will find that need to be corrected.

NOTE: Again, the bureaus are private agencies that collect information from the accounts you have relationships with. The way these accounts are listed are subject to error. By law you have the right to dispute and ensure the information being listed on your report is 100% accurate or it has to be deleted. It is up to the bureaus to investigate all of the accounts you've asked to be investigated and ensure that the creditor is giving or has given them the most accurate and up-to-date information. With that said, each dispute is not designed to ask the bureaus to investigate the accounts that are hurting you to ensure that the accounts are yours and that all the information being furnished is 100% accurate. If you know that the information on the report is correct, and it hurts your score, but you decide to dispute it anyway, this behavior is known as credit sweeping and it is illegal. Like, jail time illegal.

Once you've identified an account that is hurting you, all you have to do is plug in your information into the templates and make sure you edit the information according to your particular situation.

Preparation

When you are ready to send off your first set of letters, there are a few things you need to know. The bureaus have 30-45 days to get back to you about any dispute you make. They have sneaky ways of buying themselves more time. One of the tricks is to send you a request for identifying information. You can beat this little trick by sending in each dispute with a copy of government issued photo identification and a copy of your signed Social Security card. If you want to ensure they don't try this, send in a document like a paycheck stub or car registration with an address that matches the one on your license and matches the address to where you want them to send your correspondences. This will also help you down the line when you are disputing inaccurate and outdated addresses.

Stay Organized

Unfortunately, in many cases the dispute process is not a one-and-done process. Many times, you will have to send off the letters several times before you see a result.

To help make this dispute process seamless, here are a few pro-tips to help you stay organized.

Keep copies of your letters on a computer organized by the type of letter being sent out and the correspondence number. Example:

Main Folder

Sub Folders

Folder Contents

Every time a letter is sent, add it to its respective folder. Categorize every type of correspondence (ex. Name Correction or Verification request), and every bureau within that folder gets a folder.

Also, naming your documents to help you stay organized helps as well. The name of the document will serve as a back-up for you to know when you sent it and how far along you've come.

Here is an example of how we name our documents.

If we're saving a letter for the bureaus to verify a collections account, it will be saved as:

TransUnion – Account Verification – Date – Batch One

Shorthand: *TU_AcctVerif_012020_B1*

You will get used to it after the first few letters. Saving and storing your documents early on will save you so much time and effort later. Trust me when I tell you there is nothing worse that wondering how many correspondences you've already sent.

Here are a few more things you will need to know as you walk into the dispute process.

Once you start sending dispute letters – collection companies may begin to call more, start to send notices in the mail, or start to send you bills. They may even call your place of employment to verify information about you (yes, this has happened so many times).

There is a letter in the dispute template package telling them time to stop.

Also, you can expect to begin getting collection notices in the mail. When the bureaus conduct their investigations as a result of your dispute letter, they will send you and the company you're disputing the same notice to try to prove that the information they originally submitted to the bureaus is correct. A collection notice is not what you are asking for. Each letter contains a list of requirements you want the bureaus to investigate to determine if the information is being reflected accurately.

The Choice

When you are looking at your report, you may find a negative item that you want to dispute, but if the account will fall off in a year or two and it's a lot of money, you have a choice to make. Many have asked if they should pay if off or not and this is how I like to address this question.

Yes, it's true that the longer a collection account is on your credit, the less of an impact is has on your overall score. Yes, it is also true that most accounts fall off seven to ten years. Knowing this you have a few choices to make.

You can pay off your debt knowing that there is a possibility it may come off or you can let it fall off if it is scheduled to come off soon.

There is a downside to letting it fall off. Let's say you have a year before an account is scheduled to come off, anything can happen in that year. If you go to apply for a loan or credit, creditors or lenders may hold collection accounts against you and deny you credit. It's a risk.

I would go with having an account that is paid off (and possibly deleted) and also have the peace of mind that in case anything were to happen, my accounts are working for me and not against me. Some people choose to wait. The choice is yours now that you have the knowledge.

RULES OF THE REPAIR

Let's lay a few more ground rules before we send out our first round of letters. These rules are important because you do not want to mess up your credit while you're in the repair process.

Do Not Acquire New Credit

I feel like this should go without saying, but I am going to say it. If you are in the middle of a repair, the worst thing you can do is try to acquire new credit. New credit can throw off your score, increase the number of inquiries, change your account mix, lead to higher interest rates, alter your utilization (especially if you get and use a new credit card), and if you're late, it will impact your score negatively. New credit should not come until AFTER most or all of your negative items are removed. You'll be happy you waited.

Be Patient

Fixing your credit can take anywhere between three months to a year. How long it takes depends on how many and what kind of derogatory marks are reflected on your credit report, your current score, and the amount of debt you have. It's also important to note again that by law, the credit bureaus have at least 30 days to respond to you from the time that they get your letter. If you get impatient and keep sending letters because you haven't heard back from them in a week, you may be working against yourself. Patience is part of this process. This 30-day window can also account for why it takes so long to get your repair done. The day you plant the tree is not the same day you harvest the fruit. Please practice some patience.

Repay High Balances

Drafting a plan to repay your cards will be really important to your credit success. As stated earlier (hopefully you didn't skip that part), credit card utilization accounts for 30% of your total score. Luckily, when you pay down your card, you will get your points back. Our newsletter members receive a free interest eliminator training that outlines how to speed up this process. Making the minimum payments in this scenario isn't enough, but this training will allow you to aggressively paydown high balances and get those precious points back on your credit report. Head to www.convertedcredit.com to sign up today.

Keep Up With Bills

Do not stop paying your bills. Late payments on a loan or credit card will hurt your score more than you want to deal with during a repair. Not only that, but they are really difficult to come off of your report. This really should be rule #1. Keep paying your bills and keep paying them on time.

Do Not Ask Creditors To Lower Your Credit Limits

There are rare instances in which you may have to lower your credit limit, but during a repair this should not be something you do voluntarily. Lowering your credit limit will further put even less distance between your balance and your limit. This means your utilization will be higher. We don't want that.

Do Not Close A Card

Closing a card during a repair can have a two-punch impact if you absolutely do not have to close the card. Not only will closing a card mess with the average utilization percentage, but it will also alter the overall credit age. These are two factors that contribute to your score. Keep cards open if you can. This also applies to loan payments. If you have a loan that is close to maturity and you want to pay it off in bulk, it may actually work in your favor to spread the payments out over time as it was intended to be.

Check For Signs Of Identity Theft

There are some people who think it's okay to steal people's identities. It's really unfortunate, but it's even more unfortunate if you become a victim to one of these people. When combing through your report, here are a few signs that you may have been compromised.

- Accounts that aren't yours, but are being used

- A high number of inquiries looking into acquiring credit that you don't recognize

- Weird spellings or variations of your name

- Addresses listed that are not tied to you

- Birthdays listed that are not yours

These are just a few of the signs that you should look out for. Also consider monitoring your credit a lot more during the repair process. When your credit is improving, that could make you even more of a target. Checking regularly can help you stay ahead of anyone attempting to steal your identity.

Do Not Dispute Online Or Over The Phone

Never and I mean NEVER conduct disputes online or over the phone – always certified mail. This is the only way you can prove that you sent the letters to the bureaus. The certified mailing receipts (which you should also save and organize) will come in handy if you ever need to escalate your dispute to organizations like the Federal Trade Commission that oversees these kinds of concerns.

When sending certified, you can track certified letters, know when they got to the bureaus, and know for sure that it has landed in someone's hands since they have to be signed for. If you dispute online or over the phone, not only do you give up certain rights with online disputes, but with a phone call it's their word versus yours. If you think you will record the call, it is illegal to record without consent. Just ALWAYS send your notices certified mail as the surest way to protect yourself.

In the section that speaks about sending off letters, I will walk you through exactly how to package and send off a letter. I will also show you how to fill out a certified postal card.

Since you're a business mom, I will also show you the way I send the letters from my pajamas late at night. I'm sure you'll prefer this way.

Stay On Top Of Mail

As you send letters, you can expect to hear back from the bureaus. Be sure to open your mail and see what they have to say. In some correspondences, you may be happy to learn that some items were deleted. In other correspondences, they may be asking you to take action or send in supporting documentation. Read all of your mail and see what it says or what needs to be done. The letters you get will usually inform the next steps you have to take.

Now that you have a general idea about what you're about to do, we are getting ready to send off the first series of letters. Let's look at what we are going to send, why, and how they increase your chances of having a better score.

CHAPTER 7

Make Them Work For It

"If repairing one's credit is as easy as sending some dispute letters to the credit bureaus, then why doesn't everyone have good credit?"
– Tyler Gregory

Gregory is correct. If credit repair were just a matter of sending letters, everyone would have good credit. There are laws and loopholes I'm going to introduce to you to that will increase the chances of you actually repairing your credit and not becoming just another letter sender.

In Chapter Five, we broke down your report and the most common items you will see on there. The information outlined in Chapter Five will come in handy now. When you are sending a dispute letter, the goal of the letter is to remove the items that need verification because it may be inaccurate or incomplete. Usually, this is also information that is hurting your credit score.

Once the bureaus receive your information, they have to investigate the information you determined was inaccurate or incomplete. It's your right. If they are unable to verify the information is accurate or complete, by law, they have to remove the account from your credit report.

Simple right? Right.

However, let's consider where the credit bureaus get the information to actually validate your inquiry into an inaccurate or incomplete account.

Do you think there is a dedicated department that goes letter by letter to determine if the information is relevant or not? Nope. In most cases, there isn't even a human touching the paperwork. There is an automated system called *E-OSCAR* that goes through various data furnishers' databases to verify the information for you.

Data furnishers? Yes, data furnishers.

There are other bureaus other than the big three (Experian, Equifax, and TransUnion). The three typically do not speak to each other to communicate about the accuracy of your information. The big three will communicate with other data furnishing companies to verify the contents of your dispute.

What we do in response to the external debt validation is ask that third party personal information be suppressed. You do not know what is being reported to the big three, it is your right to have that data withheld from anyone seeking to have it, and it forces the bureaus to actually do their jobs.

I have included letter templates to the alternate bureaus that need to be reached out to.

So, before you even reach out to the big three, this is the first step. Ask the alternate bureaus to suppress your data from being shared. The time frame for suppression is usually five years, but in most cases you can ask that it is reversed via fax or letter.

Who Are The Alternate Bureaus And What Do They Do?

There are over 40 bureaus in total and all of them have the same job – store information about you.

The ones that matter most to you today are:

Bureau Name	Types of Information They Store
CoreLogic CoreScore	Rental and Credit History
Innovis	Credit History
LexisNexis	Insurance History
National Consumer Telecom and Utilities Exchange	Telecommunication and Utilities History
TeleCheck	Banking
SageStream	Credit History
Advanced Resolution Services	Credit History

After you have reached out to each of these bureaus, they have thirty days to respond to your request. It wouldn't hurt to take a photo, print-to-PDF or screenshot the confirmation that comes after you submit the request online. If you send the letters in by mail, they will send you a letter by mail confirming that they received your data suppression request.

NOTE: This is the only exception to the rule. The big three should not be disputed with or contacted online. The only time to deal with the big three online is when you are pulling your reports. That's it.

Alternate bureaus online options:

You will not need your letter templates for this, however, they will ask for additional information like proof of who you are so have that ready.

Bureau Name	Online	Mail In
CoreLogic CoreScore	https://teletrackfreeze.corelogic.com/	CoreLogic Credco, LLC P.O. Box 509124 San Diego, CA 92150
Innovis	https://www.innovis.com/securityFreeze/index	Innovis Consumer Assistance PO Box 26 Pittsburgh, PA 15230-0026
LexisNexis	https://optout.lexisnexis.com/	LexisNexis Risk Solutions Consumer Center Attn: Security Freeze P.O. Box 105108 Atlanta, GA 30348-5108
National Consumer Telecom and Utilities Exchange	*No online option*	Security Freeze Exchange Service Center – NCTUE P.O. Box 105561 Atlanta, GA 30348
Teletrack	https://teletrackfreeze.corelogic.com/	TELECHECK SERVICES, INC P.O. BOX 6806 HAGERSTOWN, MD 21741
SageStream	https://optout.lexisnexis.com/	SageStream, LLC Consumer Office, P.O. Box 503793 San Diego, CA 92150

Advanced Resolution Services	https://www.ars-consumeroffice.com/add	Advanced Resolution Services, Inc. 5005 Rockside Road, Suite 600 Independence, OH 44131

When you freeze or opt-out of having your data shared, it doesn't only impact the credit bureaus from accessing that information. If you were to apply for a new credit card (which you shouldn't be doing during the repair process anyway, remember?) the credit card company will not have access to that information as well. This will only create a delay, not necessarily a disqualification. Once you are absolutely done with the repair process, you can reach out to the bureaus again and ask that the opt-out is lifted.

Also, it may be good to know that a lot of these companies have joined forces (ex. LexisNexis and SageStream). Two sets of the links are identical, and that wasn't a mistake or typo. They have recently merged forces. I mention this because you want to ensure that when they let you know your data is frozen, it is with both, not just one of the companies.

Online Dispute Notes

When you dispute online, again, please be sure to store the confirmation in some way. Screenshot, photo, or print-to-PDF are some of the more common ways.

Check your email. In some instances, the data company may reach out to ask for additional information to verify your identity. Usually this is a utility bill. They can and or will let you know what they deem to be a valid form of identification.

Downside:

The downside to online verification is that in some cases, you will not get a notification of the suppression/freeze has been applied. You either have to go on good faith that they did their jobs or you have to keep tabs on when the 30 days are up and verify for yourself.

Upside:

You don't have to worry about mailing off several letters. Also, the online process is a little easier than writing out the information on the templates.

Paper Dispute Notes

If you choose to mail it in, please use the certified mail version. When sending in your letters, you want to be sure to add your proof of address and identification immediately. If you don't, they will take 30 days to get back to you, then you have to wait another 30 days to hear back about the information they are requesting identification verification for. Just to be safe, include copies of your license/permit (with your CURRENT mailing address), Social Security card, and a utility bill with a bill date within the last 30 days and with an address that matches the address on your license.

If for some reason you don't have this information, attach a different verification document and add a note at the bottom of your letter stating that the document you attached is all you have to prove you are who you say you are.

Other acceptable forms of proof of address (in order from greatest to least)

- Credit card statement face sheet

- Paycheck stubs

- Lease agreement/mortgage statement

- Bank reference

- Voter registration card

- Tax return face sheet

- Bank statement face sheet

Upside:

One of the benefits to sending the letter in the mail is the option to track. If you have been really reading the book, you can tell how important keeping a paper trail is to me. Sending mail certified is an official paper trail because you are sending it through the United States Postal Service.

Another upside is that you will get a correspondence in the mail letting you know that your freeze/opt-out has been initiated. Hold on to this paperwork for up to two years in case you ever need to prove that you indeed asked for one.

Downside:

The major downsides to sending the letters via mail is the cost and the time it will take to get the letter prepared. You will have to send the letters to each bureau individually. Certified letters can range from a little under $5.00 and, with the tool I will share with you later, they can go for about $8 per letter. It is a small investment to make, but an important one that may cause a slight inconvenience if you are not willing to spend the money.

CHAPTER 8

Making The Templates Work For You

Y ou understand what's hurting your score, you've sent your freeze request off and confirmed it's frozen, now what?

Well, now is the time to pull your report and start filling in the templates with what you want the bureaus to investigate.

There are a variety of templates to choose from, but the one that fits your particular need is the one that can be used. This requires reading the title of the template and the body to see if this addresses what you need.

I understand that some situations are not one size fits all, so please feel free to alter the templates as you need to, to make sure it fits your particular need.

Collections Dispute Letters

This is a good opportunity to state that this is not to be taken as legal advice since I am not a lawyer. The templates simply outline the consumer laws that the bureaus are violating by having inaccurate or incomplete information on your credit report. This is information you are more than welcome to and encouraged to look up online.

If you need a consumer rights attorney for more detailed or legal advice on how to deal with the bureaus (there are cases when this is appropriate), then you should seek legal counsel.

Why These Templates Are Effective

The consumer laws work in a way that if the bureaus undergo their investigation and cannot substantially prove the information is complete or accurate, it must be removed. That's the law. Some people ask if this is like getting off on a "technicality" – I do not believe so. Unfortunately, there is only so much you can see on a report and there is a lot of information that is being hidden from you. The letters ask for an in-depth investigation into the information you can't see. It demands accountability to the information that may be harming you that hasn't been substantiated. This is your consumer right.

If the bureaus conduct their investigation and determine that everything is being reported correctly and completely, then we are happy they have done their job and we move on to Phase Two.

Another unique feature of these templates is that they are broken down into four rounds. I don't think you personally need more than four rounds to get the job done. Sometimes it takes more, but those methods are super aggressive and should be overseen by a trained professional, so you don't open up yourself to the chance of being exposed to a lawsuit.

With each letter, the demands change slightly to meet the result the bureaus send, so look out for changes in the templates round for round.

Increasing Your Chance Of Success

The bureaus will do anything to buy more time to investigate. There are legal loopholes that they will use to get 60 sometimes even 90 days to complete one investigation request.

Loophole 1: "Verify" Your Identity

In some cases the bureaus will send you a letter back within 30 days stating that they need more information to verify your identity. In most cases, they don't really even need the additional information, they just ask for it to maintain the 30-day compliance while they continue to investigate. This is why it is crucial to send in a copy of your driver's license (with current address), a copy of your Social Security card, and a utility bill. This can help to prove your identity.

Get ahead of this trick by sending in as much identifying information as you can to avoid this little tricky loophole.

Loophole 2: Satisfactory Investigation With No Proof

Yet another stall tactic. In some cases the bureaus will let you know that they investigated the items you requested be investigated and found that the information was indeed yours without sending any proof. Instead, they will send a new report because they have to by law, but that is not what you asked for. The second letter can include information stating just that or whatever they claimed the reason was that the accounts were satisfactorily investigated.

They may also determine that after the four rounds they will not investigate again, with still no proof.

You have two options at this point:

a. Escalate to the Federal Trade Commission (FTC)

This option means compiling copies of all the correspondences (rounds one to four) that you sent to the bureaus, copies of the certified receipts, and copies of corresponding letters the bureau sent (relative to the rounds), and ship them off to the Federal Trade Commission.

I've included a template you can attach that goes on top of the items you're mailing off to the FTC.

NOTE: the FTC template letter must be signed and should also include proof of your identification.

At this point, you will have to wait to see what they say. Once you get their feedback you will know how to proceed.

b. Negotiate and settle debts

Negotiations and settlements are opportunities you can seize to pay off the debt at a reduced amount. The ideal negotiation leaves you only having to pay 40-50% of the original debt amount.

I split the ideas of negotiations and settlements into two categories for a reason. For the sake of this process, I'll define negotiations as a fixed reduced cost you pay in one transaction for the collection or charge off account.

On the other hand, let's look at a settlement as debt that is broken down into smaller digestible payments, but you are still paying the total amount the bureaus determined was accurately being reported.

Some companies will tell you that they won't budge on the price; however, remind them that you called them and you do want it resolved. In some cases, if they won't budge on the price, ask if they have a hardship program.

For either a negotiation or a settlement, the end goal is to have the negative account's influence on your score to end.

In many cases, if you agree to a negotiation or a settlement, the collection company will let you know that they will no longer report the collection account to the creditors. That is their right to stop reporting. However, the waters get a little murky when you ask that the collection account is no longer being reported as a result of a payment being made by you.

You can ask, but they don't have to oblige. In many cases, once they get their money, they don't want to pay to report your information to the credit bureaus anymore anyway and the negative item can fall off sooner than the seven to ten years it may take.

We have attached a letter template you can send off with your payment that asks the collection company to stop reporting the negative items once repayment of the debt is satisfied. Again, it's up to them, but the goal is that they are no longer reporting the account as delinquent so that your credit can be spotless.

Loophole 3: Request For More Information

In addition to the bureaus stating that they cannot verify your identity or that they satisfactorily verified your information (despite the lack of proof), they may send a letter saying that they will no longer reinvestigate and that the only way they will investigate again is if you send more proof that supports your claims. This is a trap.

The way you can address this is to call them out on it. Plain and simple. Other stall tactics include but aren't limited to:

- A correspondence that my say your disputes are suspicious

- Your account has been updated but you see no change

- Claims that your disputes are "frivolous"

- A notice stating that they think you're working with a credit repair company

When people get these letters, they get discouraged or they feel like the process doesn't work. This is exactly the time to circle back to the mindset piece we discussed at length in the first half of the book. Trust the process.

More On Negotiations

We touched on a few key points regarding negotiations, but I would be remiss to not mention some important information that can help you make up your mind moving forward. Negotiations and settlements are the options we use if the bureaus have done their investigations and found (actually found) that everything is being reported accurately and completely.

NOTE (especially for collections): Collection companies are companies that purchase your debt at a fraction of the cost from the alleged original company they claim you had business with. When you call them, please know that they are attempting to collect on a debt that they paid pennies on the dollar for and when they collect they are turning a profit.

When negotiating with the collection companies, DO NOT TELL THEM HOW MUCH YOU ARE WILLING TO PAY. Ask them what is the least amount of money they are willing to accept for the collection account and then drop that number by 20%-30%. If you are speaking to someone who insists they can't do it, ask if there is someone else you can speak with that can get the job done (supervisor, manager, superior – whatever).

What you should do is walk into the conversation with a dollar in mind that you do not wish to go above. Please be reasonable here. These are businesses and they are in the business of making money.

If you are at the point where you realize a settlement is your best bet, here are a few steps that have made the process seamless for others. If it's a debt you can afford to pay upfront, still negotiate the price.

1. If it's a larger debt that you may have to break up into smaller payments over time, before you make your first payment, get the terms in writing.

By terms I mean:

- Number of payments

- Penalties for missing a payment (usually this means not being able to create another payment arrangement with them, so make sure the amount agreed upon is an amount you can manage financially before you begin).

- Agree to stop reporting when final payment is made

With either payment, when the final payment is made, you want to send in the final payment with a letter in the template section that reiterates their agreement to stop reporting and processing the payment solidifies that agreement.

When you call, there are key pieces of information you will need to collect to fill in this template properly so I've also included the log that you will need to document the items in preparation for that letter.

All in all, be prepared for this call to the collection companies by having your call template handy and the attitude of fighting for your finances. In the next chapter, I want to outline some of the most common errors you will see on your report. These are important because spotting these errors can greatly impact your overall results.

CHAPTER 9

Ethical Considerations

Over the years, the question of ethics comes into play around credit repair because the potential for abuse is abundant. There are people out there who use these very powerful tools and letters to intentionally default on accounts and then clean up their credit again. They may also engage in some other shady credit methods that allow them to assume an entirely new identity.

This is not the goal here.

In 2013, the Federal Trade Commission reported that one in five people can spot an error on their credit reports. I have seen hundreds of consumer reports and there are less than 3% of them that do not have an error.

Unfortunately, on the business side, if a company were to gain the tools to report on your behalf, they may report a collection and try to collect on debt that you don't even really owe. This scam isn't unheard of and is very possible. Small details like this go unnoticed and can absolutely harm your ability to maintain a great score and look favorable to lenders.

Agencies like the Federal Trade Commission and the Consumer Financial Protection Bureau (among others) are created to protect you and hold you accountable. There are also laws that are meant to protect you from unscrupulous practices. This is why there are a few areas where case law is referenced within the letters.

When an item is inaccurate or incomplete, it must go. The bureaus are private (not government organizations) that are held to laws meant to ensure reporting is correct.

When you are looking for inaccurate or incomplete items, here are a few of the most common:

Personal Information Errors

- Incorrect name, address, or place of employment

- Merged accounts – accounts that are not yours but may be for someone with a similar name

- Accounts opened as a result of identity theft

Account Status Errors

- Closed accounts being reported as open and vice versa

- Being listed as an primary owner on an account where you are an authorized user

- Accounts that are regularly reported as late, but it's an error

- Dates reported incorrectly (last payment, date opened, or date of delinquency) on report

- Duplicate debt accounts

Balance Errors

- Current balance isn't being reported correctly

- Credit limit is being reported inaccurately

Data Furnishing Errors

- Placement of accounts that were already deleted or removed

- Accounts that are past their removal date (two years inquiry and seven-to-ten years other delinquencies)

- Duplicate accounts listed incorrectly (different collection companies, no name on one and name on other, etc.)

These are just some of the most common I've seen throughout the years, however, it isn't just limited to these few. If you're unsure, this would be a great opportunity to reach out to a professional or join a group like the Converted Community on Facebook. When you don't know, a moderator or someone with a similar situation can answer your question. I want to be sure you don't miss out on having potentially harmful information on your credit report because you're unsure of where to go for help.

Again, errors are very common. They are also very harmful since they can misrepresent you as a potential lending consumer. Dig through the templates to see which one best fits your situation and map out how you are going to go about attacking these errors.

In the next chapter, I want to give you a few pointers on mistakes to avoid when going through the dispute process. These are important because these warnings will greatly impact how you approach the credit repair process. Please do not skip over the upcoming chapter, you've already made it this far. The next chapter will help you optimize your results.

CHAPTER 10

A Cautionary Tale- How Credit Repair Can Hurt You

I t's really important to know that as much as this repair process can help your score, it can hurt your score and you as well.

Let's go over some the steps you need to be mindful of to avoid mistakes, avoid seeing huge fluctuations in your score, and a few things you should know and understand through the process.

Ignoring Notices

The most common mistake that people make that should be avoided is ignoring notices that come in the mail. Gone are the days of debtor prisons, however, it is not uncommon to receive a legal notice from a law firm that is working on behalf of a debtor.

Ignoring these lawsuits or court hearings can mean having your wages garnished or a lien being put on your bank account.

The collection company has one goal – to collect. They are willing to work with you as long as you are willing to work with them. As a matter of fact, if you are experiencing a legitimate hardship that makes it difficult to pay, this would be a good time to present this information in front of a judge. Whatever you do, do not ignore those notices. They are very real with very real consequences.

Other notices that often go ignored are the ones from collection companies. In some cases, when collection companies are asked to prove they are truly owed, they may do away with the account all together since they know they will not be able to fulfill the documentation requested in the investigation. The result of the investigation drives them to do away with the collection account altogether.

Side Bar: This is one more reason to keep an eye on your mail. The collection company may communicate with you to let you know it is being removed. On the other hand, a collection company may reach out to you in order to deceive you or to try to threaten you into paying. This is illegal.

The Fair Debt Collection Practice Act (FDCPA) makes it really clear about what debt collectors can and can't do.

Here are a few things to look out for (and why you shouldn't ignore the calls per se):

- They have to identify themselves and let you know that they are attempting to collect a debt owed

- They have to tell you the name of the original creditor, what you owe, and how you can dispute/validate the debt

- They cannot talk to your employer, friends, or family about the debt

- They have a limit on the number of times they can call you daily

- They cannot insult or threaten you

- They cannot call you after you've requested they stop calling you

- They cannot use deceptive, misleading, or inaccurate information in their correspondences

If you find that any debt collector is guilty of these FDCPA violations and you can prove the collection company was in the wrong, you can sue for up to $1,000 per violation. In some cases you may even be able to get your legal fees covered. One more reason to keep good records and ensure you are not ignoring those correspondences.

If you're not sure a violation has occurred, reach out to a local consumer rights attorney. In most cases, they will not ask for money upfront. They can and most often will take a percentage of what you win in court as payment.

The collector may also reach out to you to let you know that they are extending a settlement offer for less than you even anticipate paying. The collection company will give you 30 days to answer the offer as well as let you know how they will accept the payment. You can still use the good will adjustment strategy and template to ask the collector to stop reporting the collection to the bureaus upon payment.

Not Staying On Top of Letters

Similar to ignoring notices is not staying on top of your letters. Remember, within 30 days of sending a dispute notice, the bureaus have to send you a notice responding to your investigation request. Within that notice sent by the bureaus, they will be letting you know what the result of your dispute was. If an item is removed, you can move on to the next steps. If nothing has changed, you will know that it's time to move on to round two, three, or four. If you don't stay on top of those notices, you can miss out on valuable time needed to correspond with the bureaus.

Staying on top of your letters looks like:

- Staying organized

- Keeping return receipts

- Tracking when letters get to the bureaus

- Looking through letters for results

- Setting a time to follow-up with bureaus or collectors

This is a time game and you don't want to lose any more of it. Stay on top of your letters so you can position yourself to beat the clock and win.

Disputing All items

Not every item on your credit report is created equal. I have seen clients dispute positive items that were helping their score only to have it removed. Their score suffered because of it. For the most part, the most important items to dispute are the items that haven't been verified as accurate and the ones that are hurting your score that could contain incomplete information.

Also, one really important reason not to dispute everything is because the bureaus will shrug off your request as "erroneous." Literally, the letter will say this is an erroneous dispute. In a way they are kind of right. Everything can't be wrong. Dispute only what you need to, to increase your odds of success.

Closing A Card

A commonly innocent mistake that many consumers make when fixing their credit independently is closing a credit card. The idea is that if the card is not being used, then there is no need to keep it. In theory, this makes sense, but in practice we learned that this card may actually be keeping your credit score elevated. Closing a card may hurt you. Let's break it down.

A credit card addresses four of the five elements of your credit score.

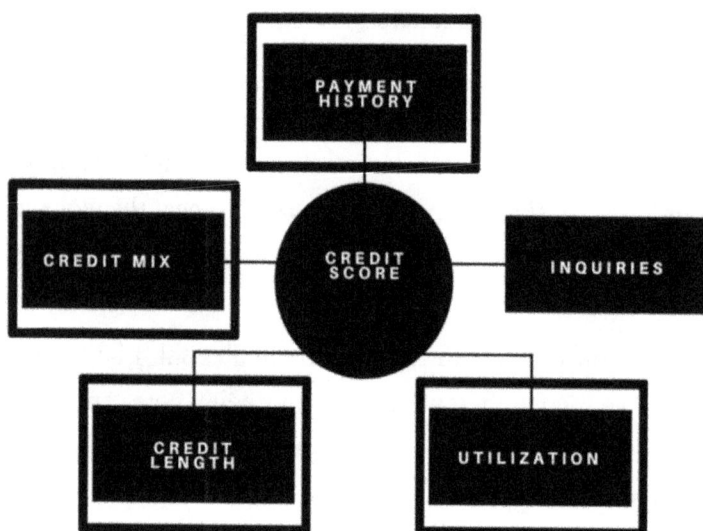

When you remove a positive account you are knocking off a lot of positive history that can take years to get back. We already know how important all of these factors are from the breakdown earlier in the book. Do not lose precious points. Keep your cards open for now. If they have high balances, pay them down. They will benefit you later (I'll explain more in the resource section).

Trying To Get New Credit

I honestly feel like I shouldn't have to say this, but I've seen it so many times that it is worth a mention. During the repair is not the time to try to take on new credit. The time will come, just not during the repair stage.

When you try to take on new credit at the wrong time, you add inquiries to your credit report, you risk getting denied, and even if you are approved, your interest rates will still be high.

After your credit is cleaned up, you can take the initiative to get new credit if you need it.

Not Maintaining Proof

Keeping your paperwork is the only way to prove you reached out to the bureaus or collection companies. It isn't uncommon for them to claim they didn't get any letters from you. Your return receipt is your proof. It's your word against theirs. The more proof you have and the more coordinated your paper trail, the better.

No Late Payments

Also, again it should go without saying, but there is a misconception that existing accounts do not need to be attended to when you are repairing your credit. Continue to operate like an ideal credit consumer even if you are in the process of disputing.

Continue to pay on time or you will see your score drop significantly.

Sending Fake Documents

Sometimes, the bureaus will reach out to you asking you for information to support your claim. DO NOT (I repeat) DO NOT SEND DOCTORED OR FAKE DOCUMENTS. This can get you in a lot of trouble in addition to being illegal.

Some people feel as if they have to resort to this option because they do not have the information being requested, but if this is the case, default to escalating your case to the FTC. Let the Federal Trade Commission take care of it.

Overall, the goal is to keep you from inadvertently hurting your score when the objective is to help it. If you make these crucial mistakes you may see your score drop, take longer to have your credit improved, and see major score fluctuations.

Now, we will explore the resources that we need to rebuild your credit and thereby set your family up for an incredible financial future.

CHAPTER **11**

Resources & Recommendations

There was an announcement at the end of 2020 that President Joe Biden wants to partner with the Consumer Financial Protection Bureau (CFPB) to overhaul the entire credit system. There are tons of articles online about the proposed basics, but the most important takeaway is that if your credit isn't good before those changes are implemented, it will be nearly impossible to correct later.

This entire section is designed to break down some of the new technologies that are emerging with the times that are coming. If you find that any of these resources are not a fit for you, look into the category or similar products that can fit your particular needs.

NOTE: I want to remind you that in order to get the best results when implementing these resources, your credit should be cleaned up first. If you try to add some of these resources with derogatory items still listed, you may not see significant improvements to your score.

Let's look at some resources, how to apply them, and how they will impact your score.

Secured Cards

Secured cards get a bad rap. They have been stigmatized, but they shouldn't. Secured cards are cards that you have to put some money on as collateral. The bank will give you a credit card for the amount of money that you use to "secure" the card and if you carry a balance, you will be paying interest on your own money. Paying interest on your own money is what people hate the most, but if you work your credit correctly, you shouldn't carry a balance.

Also, many card companies are encouraging consumers to get a secured card and after a year or so of proper usage they will either give you the money back or extend you an unsecured card, by extending an unsecured card (no money/collateral card) after one year of positive use of the secured card. In some instances, the card company may also apply your "security" to a new unsecured credit limit (higher than what you initially put down to get the credit card).

To begin, I don't think anyone needs more than two secured cards because they are a means to an end. They are basic cards that need to report your payment history to the credit bureaus and reward you for using them. That's it. Once your score has increased, you can move on to unsecured cards that do cool things like points, rewards, and cash back percentages (that's how you get paid to use your credit card).

Most secured cards will pull a hard inquiry when you apply for one; so, please keep this in mind if you already have a ton of inquiries that are unrelated. Remember, any inquiries over four will hurt your score. If I were in the market for a secured card, I would shop around to find out what the approval requirements are. The goal is to ensure I meet as many of their standards as possible.

Discover

First card you can look into is the Discover "Discover It" Secured card. I personally like to suggest this card to my clients because Discover lets you start with a $200 deposit. That $200 will become the limit you can access and what the bureaus will see. Good credit practices means using only 20% of the balance at any given time, no late payments, and no defaulting. After a year of consistent credit interactions, Discover usually refunds you the $200 you used to secure the card and offers you a $1200 line of unsecured credit.

Consider the $200 a small upfront investment to make to build your credit. The creditor essentially uses your money to minimize their risk and stablish faith with you as a borrower.

Why We Love It:

- No annual fee

- Great consumer reviews

- Low entry requirements

- Has rewards

If you decide to use this card, there are many great benefits with virtually no downsides. Like all of the other information in this book, you are invited to look more into the option that is the best fit for you.

Chime

Chime is revolutionary because they are getting with the times. Chime realizes that the credit card game is about to change. They have offered consumers a way to acquire credit and build their credit with no interest whatsoever. As a consumer who may have had credit card debt in the past, this is an attractive option to you. This may also be attractive to "new to credit" consumers that are afraid to get into credit cards because of the debt risk.

Features

No annual fee

No interest

No security deposit required

No credit checks (so no inquiries)

No utilization reported

Downsides:

Need Chime spending account to access card (it's a free account)

Leverage your own money to build credit

The overall upside of this card is that it helps you with payment history (35% of your total score). It may also benefit someone with high debt usage that doesn't want to add to it. In a way, the Chime card acts as a secured card, but without the same underwriting requirements of a traditional creditor. They are reporting whatever you put on your card, your payment behavior, your credit mix, and history will all benefit from these types of cards.

Cleo

This card isn't just granted to everyone. Unlike Chime, you have to qualify for it.

Once you've opened a paid spending account, you upload money from your spend account, and that is the limit you have to work with.

Cleo also has a small interest rate, a paid spending account, and other features within that paid account that let you budget/save money automatically.

Cleo wants to act as your bank and your credit card at the same time. When you open an account with them, they pull your bank information to suggest budgeting options you can use and they also have features that allow you to create a savings plan. After your bank data is analyzed, then and only then will they potentially offer you a secured credit card.

Even if you aren't extended credit with Cleo, it may be worth exploring this account with them based on some of the other features they have.

Self-Lender

Every time I present this option to somebody, they're like, what's the catch? No catch. This is the number one resource out there, and I've been using it since 2017. I still have an account with them.

Every time they send me my money back, I use the fund to open a new account with them. Why? Because it's just that good. The service I'm speaking of is called Self. You might have used them before or heard of them in the past; they were formerly "Self-Lender."

Self is a credit builder loan. Loans are hard to come by, especially personal loans. With account mix being one of the elements of your credit score, your ability to have loans and credit cards matter in the process of improving your score. So Self is playing on the account mix element of your credit score and helping you get that slight bump by creating an account for you that reflects on your credit report as a loan. The account isn't actually a loan but a Certificate of Deposit (CD). Every time you pay into the CD, they're reporting a positive on-time payment, this payment will be applied to the payment history on your credit report. The best feature (in my opinion) is that each payment is being saved for you in that CD.

First, Self is creating the CD for you in the amount you decide you want to pay every month from their options. With every payment you pay, it goes into a CD. This CD lets you save up the total amount of money you agreed to pay monthly for the term you choose.

For example, you can choose a credit-builder account for $25 a month. It costs $9 to activate the account, and that's the only fee outside of the money that you're going to pay monthly. If you choose the $25 plan, you'll pay that for 24 months and at the end of that time you would have saved $520.

Every $25 payment is reporting on your credit report and adds to positive payment history. When your "loan" is "paid," they will give you the option to cash out the $520 (get it back into your hands) or you can apply that amount to a credit card they will open for you through the Self platform.

This option is best for people who have little history, need an account mix, or they are trying to add positive payment history. This is also for anyone who is interested in saving and building their credit simultaneously.

Self is one of my favorite options.

Like all the other options presented, this works best if you are not acquiring new late payments and after your credit has been cleaned up. The only downside to this account is that if you don't pay (like any other account) it will negatively impact your credit. Be sure that when you want to exhaust this option, you are ready to begin.

Report Your Rent

Another great option that a lot of people don't know about is that you can report your rent and sometimes utilities to the credit bureaus. If you are a renter, this is going to be great for you. Most of the programs I am going to share with you have a fee, they will let you report to one, two, or all the major bureaus, and they will report your past (usually up to two years) or ongoing rental history.

This is a great option because rent is one of those necessary evils. We must pay it anyway, why not get the added benefit of having a credit score boost?

Of course, there are downsides.

Some of these companies do not report to all three bureaus so you may have to combine a few resources together to get the best results to your credit score. The bureaus that are most reported to are Equifax and TransUnion. Some people offset the discrepancies they will see in their Experian score by adding Experian Boost.

Rent Reporting Programs:

Program Name	Reports To	Benefit
Rent Reporters	TransUnion and Equifax	Adds to payment history Adds to credit age Average of 40 points earned Quick results Provides credit scores
Renal Kharma	TransUnion and Equifax	No credit check Average of 40 points earned Quick results Adds payment history Adds credit age Partner or Spouse can add to credit as well
Level Credit	Equifax and TransUnion	Identity theft protection Reports utility payments as well as rent Adds payment history Adds credit age
Rock the Score	TransUnion primarily and Equifax with exceptions	Partner or Spouse can add to credit as well Adds payment history Adds credit age
Esusu Rent	All three bureaus	Adds payment history Adds credit age Average of 47 points earned Credit score and credit report options

	Equifax and TransUnion	Adds payment history
CreditMyRent		Adds credit age
		Easy enrollment
PaymentReport	Equifax and TransUnion	Adds payment history Adds credit age Partner or Spouse can add to credit as well

Look into:

Program Name	Company	Benefits
Experian Boost	Experian	Adds utility and other subscription-like payments to your credit report

The second downside, which is not great, your landlord has to get on board with this. They don't have to do any of the reporting, but they do have to agree to sign up to the programs and make slight adjustments as to how they are paid and sometimes when they are paid.

In some cases, you would have to explain the program to the landlord if they're not already familiar with rent reporting and ask them if that's an option they can work with on your behalf because it is an option that you can benefit from.

Please note, most of the rent reporting companies only report to two of the bureaus – usually TransUnion and Equifax. If you want to use this, you may benefit from adding Experian Boost to level off the score discrepancies that are bound to happen.

Authorized Users (AU)

This is one of my least favorite methods, not because it doesn't work, but because of how much it is abused.

The option to add yourself as an authorized user on someone's card is called "piggy backing." Essentially, if you know someone with really great credit cards (pays on time, low balance, good age), you can be added to that card as an authorized user and have their positive credit history reflected on to yours through that card.

Sounds amazing, right? Right.

You get the benefit of someone's good credit behavior by being added to their card. The problem is, many people abuse this option by adding themselves to a ton of cards or, worse, buying access to someone's card, and it puts them in worse off situations than when they started.

This section I'll dedicate to breaking down best uses for an AU card and reasons why you shouldn't just pile them on.

- You absolutely positively should NEVER PAY FOR AN AUTHORIZED USER SLOT.

- Also, an absolute rule is, you must trust the individual you are asking for the AU slot. If this person happens to max out that card, miss a payment, or close the card, your score will feel the impact of all those actions. You can remove the slot, but it is not as easy as being added.

- Debt to income. If you plan on financing something, this is for you. When the lender goes to calculate your debt-to-income ratio, there is a good chance that they may use the authorized user information to make that calculation. I have had clients rack up ten-to-twelve tradelines, get 100 points, but then get denied in underwriting because over half of their income was swallowed up by debt (that wasn't even theirs). Just don't do it. There is no prize for trying to game the system. AUs are a tool, nothing more nothing less.

- Repair first: if you try to pile on AUs to a credit report riddled with negative items, it is not going to be as effective. Your credit report needs to be nearly spotless for this to work.

How to ask family or friends for an AU slot:

- Let them know that there is nothing you can do to harm their credit. As a matter of fact, they can do harm to your score.

- You do not need a card for this to work but if one is issued, cut it up.

- Let them know that you are using this option temporarily to improve your credit. Once you get the score you need and are able to get your own cards, they can remove you. Ultimately, it is not a permanent decision.

  o The best card they can put you on would be between five-to-seven years old, has a utilization below 30% (the lower the better), and has no late payments or no late payments at least in the last two years.

- Ask that you are informed of any changes they are going to make (max out card, close the card, or unable to pay). The only reason you need to know is so that you can remove yourself before your score feels the impact.

Lastly, this tip is for you (the asker). Make sure this is someone you trust implicitly because they will have your full name, Social Security number, and in some cases your address. This is more than enough information to have your identity stolen. Be sure you trust this individual.

Subprime Merchandise Accounts

This is also one of my least favorite options, but not because it's not effective. It's just not the best, but it does have its place for certain people.

Subprime accounts are lines of credit or loans that are offered very easily. The reason subprime accounts are attractive is because they are meant to attract individuals with subprime credit. It can be used as a credit building tool, but without the right credit education, subprime borrowers are opening themselves up to high interest rates and unnecessary debt.

Subprime borrowers like this option because subprime accounts usually have easy approvals/no credit check, offer high limits, and can help them build their credit if used properly. This option also offers you a little bit more control than an AU.

For example, someone looking to lower their credit utilization by adding a $10,000 line of credit would benefit from adding a subprime account; however, if you access the entire $10,000 then it defeats the entire purpose and you're now an additional $10,000 in the hole.

The downside to using this kind of credit other than debt exposure is the money you have to spend to keep the account open. Most credit companies can or will close your card to a lack of activity, but these accounts are far limited with their purchasing requirements.

Sending Your Letters From Home

I haven't forgotten. Here is how I am able to do all of this in my pajamas, at any hour of the day, and get back to the bureaus immediately.

I use an online mailing service called **Letter Stream**. It is easy to use and you can send your certified mail letters through this platform as well. It is safe to use, effective, and allows you to send letters at your convenience. Also, you have the added benefit of being able to see when your letters went out and use the tracking information to track your letters.

I couldn't include every single credit resource available because this book would take on a new life, however, we do have a weekly converted club mailing list that shares resources and credit news we think it's important for you to know. Sign up at www.convertedcredit.com

I highly encourage you to do some research! Even though I've used these strategies for other people, I want you to look into your options and make a decision that works for you. So please do your research and ask questions.

Now that you've added the resources that work best for you, let's talk about maintenance. This is the most important aspect of keeping your credit great after it's repaired and getting to the coveted FICO 800 club.

CHAPTER 12

Maintaining your New and Improved Score

We are back to the drawing board. Consider this a full circle moment. All of the concepts from the first part of the book are going to be applied to not only improve your credit, but to maintain your credit moving forward.

Also, I want you to consider that you are now where you were when you started the book, and you are closer to where you want to be. You are now informed; you possess the power to make the best and informed decisions about your credit.

The typical FICO score ranges from 300 to 850 and is calculated based on these main five factors.

- Payment History

- Debt Usage

- Length Of History

- Account Mix

- Hard Inquiries

Whenever you make a credit decision, you are either going against or moving toward points that will impact your credit score.

Only 20% of Americans have a score of 800 or higher. This is a low number, but if you make decisions considering the five factors, with time, you can be in the 800 club as well.

The 20% of Americans that consistently maintain a score of 800 or higher consistently have zero late payments. This will matter for you moving forward. Consider that the impact of a late payment greatly diminishes after two years. If you have late payments now, after two years and years forward with no late payments, you can put yourself in position to improve your score.

When it comes to debt usage, an individual with an 800 credit score does not use up more than 5% of their available credit. The 800 members also have a great mix of credit. On a credit report with an 800 credit score you will see loans (personal, auto, mortgage, student) and credit (retail, credit, lines of credit).

800 club members also plan their finances strategically. They understand that using a credit card is not a purchase for now, but a purchase that is extended long into the future. These individuals will have credit cards that are opened for 10, 20, 30, 50 years and maintain them overtime. When they have to assume new credit, they plan it out so that they do not have to face the sometimes harsh penalties of acquiring too many inquiries, accessing too much credit, and opening up their debt exposure.

If you were paying attention to how the people in the 800 club move, they use all of the five factors consistently. They plan and no decision is made without consulting the five factors.

This is what I want for you. All financial decisions are going to be a strategy. Credit is not for now– it's forever. Like many individuals, you never know when you will need to access your good credit for a major life decision.

Maintaining Your Credit Score

Visit Your Credit Report Often

Aim for reviewing your credit report once a month. Also consider setting up alerts and notifications. This will allow you to get ahead of anything unsavory that pops up.

Add Payment Reminders

Did you know that most people miss payments because they forgot? Setting up payment reminders will help you to stay on top of payments and avoid unnecessary late payments.

Pay Your Balances More Than Once A Month

If you pay your credit cards twice or three times a month, you are going to pay down your debt quickly, save on interest, and you get the bonus of keeping your utilization low.

Get New Credit Cautiously

In my mind new credit has to be justified and justified again. Planning new credit is the only way to ensure you are not getting new credit unnecessarily.

Keep Cards Open As Long As You Can

There is only one exception to closing a card. If you have high balances on your card, you may want to consider a balance transfer card. Balance transfer cards allow you to close your current card(s) and transfer your balance(s) to a new card. The benefit of doing this is the idea that most balance transfer cards offer an introductory period of 12-18 months interest free. With this card, you can plan to pay down your credit cards aggressively without any interest in the introductory period and save thousands of dollars in the meantime. The downside is that you have to close your previous cards with this high balance(s). You would have to take a bit of a hit to your credit score if those previous cards had a good credit age. Luckily, with new cards that you open and keep aged, you will get your points back with time.

I understand balance transfers are not available for everyone, so I regularly send free trainings and tools to members of the Converted Club. This training is an alternative to something like a balance transfer. I will show you how to pay down your cards aggressively and quickly. You can sign up for the Converted Club on www.convertedclub.com.

For example, the interest eliminator training will show you how to categorize your cards and shows you which ones to pay down first. It also shows you exactly how long it will take to pay off your cards using the minimum balances versus using the repayment methods outlined in the training.

Live Within Your Means

I know a budget is the real "B" word but, think of it this way: what you don't gain control of will ultimately control you. When you know what's coming in and what's going out, you can see exactly where you are burning money. You can also see where there are opportunities to optimize your funds.

Having a budget allows you to tap into high level strategies that can get you paid to use your credit card(s). For example, my credit cards are rewards cards and I set up my budget in a way that allows for most of my living expenses to be paid on my credit card. Within a week of using the card, I pay it right back, get my points, rewards, and or money. In my best year, my card paid me a total of $1,200. This is just one power of a budget.

I've been asked why I began my work on credit and the reason is because I learned that the discipline needed to really level up financially is largely due to getting discipline around your credit first. Credit is where money begins. Once you sort out your credit, the doors of money possibilities really begin to unfold.

I am sad to say that the book has come to an end. It has been my utmost pleasure sharing this knowledge with you. Final thought is please don't give up on the process. You are not alone in this struggle. If you feel like you need support, do not hesitate to reach out online to our Converted Community on Facebook or via e-mail at support@convertedcredit.com

You got this, mama! You've done harder things by bringing kids into this world, raising them to be decent people, and you've done it alone. Your capacity and bravery are already evident. Tap into this power to tackle your credit. I have complete faith in you.

APPENDIX

Best Use Notification

Please review each template carefully to see which one will work best to meet your individual needs.

Please use these templates as a general guideline. For best results, edit to meet your unique circumstances. Please double-check all templates before you send them off.

[DATE]

Credit Reporting Bureau
City, State, Zip

RE: REQUEST FOR CREDIT REPORT

To Whom It May Concern:

Please regard this as an official request to send me a copy of my credit report. Use the following information to identify me:

Name:

SS#:

Address:

City, State, Zip:

Birthdate:

Past residences (last five years):

Former Name(s)

Enclosed is $_____ as payment for the credit report.

If you have any questions, please contact me at (XXX) XXX-XXXX.

Thank you.

Sincerely,

[YOUR FULL NAME]

[Enclosures]

[DATE]

Credit Reporting Bureau
City, State, Zip

RE: REQUEST FOR FREE CREDIT REPORT

To Whom It May Concern:

I recently applied for credit, but my application was denied. I have attached the letter I received of the denial within the last 60 days. According to the document attached, the information used in the lending decision came from your bureau.

The Fair Credit Reporting Act has a provision that states that your credit bureau must send me all information on file that led to my credit application being denied. As you know, there should be no charge or fee for this information.

Please send my credit report to the address below. The attached letter contains additional information needed to confirm my identity.

If you have any questions or need additional information, please contact me at the address provided below.

Thank you.

Sincerely,

YOUR FULL NAME
ADDRESS
ADDRESS

[Enclosures]

[DATE]

FULL NAME
ADDRESS
ADDRESS
SSN

CREDIT BUREAU
ADDRESS
ADDRESS

RE: VALIDATION OF ACCOUNTS

To Whom It May Concern:

Please regard this letter as a formal request to commence an investigation regarding the potentially harmful items outlined in this letter.

I neither affirm, nor deny any purported debt you claim I owe to the listed companies.

This letter is being sent to you in response to an entry made on my credit report. Please be advised that this is not a refusal to pay the debt, but a notice sent pursuant to the Fair Debt Collection Practices Act, that your claim that I owe you money is being disputed, and validation is requested for the alleged debts listed.

Under the Fair Credit Reporting Act, I have the right to request validation of the debt being reported as owed, charged off, in collections, or any other remark in kind. Please regard this as a formal request for the physical verification of the original signed consumer contract for any and all accounts I request to be investigated that you have posted on my credit report. If this information is not furnished, it is possible that anyone paying to furnish data could be sending in my information fraudulently.

This is a request for proof that I am the right person and that there is a documented contractual obligation which is binding on me to the account being reported. Please note, this is NOT a request for "verification" via E-Oscar or proof of my mailing address, but a request for VALIDATION made per the Fair Debt Collection Practices Act. Proof is quantified by an original Consumer Contract with my Signature on it. Your inability to produce this information could affect my ability to obtain credit.

Reporting inaccurate and unsubstantiated information to a credit reporting agency may constitute as fraud under federal law (FCRA). Compliance with this request is required per the laws of my state and per federal laws that all unverifiable accounts must be removed and if you are unable to provide me a copy of verifiable proof, you must remove the accounts listed below:

Account	Account Number	Provide Physical Verification
ACCOUNT NAME	XXXXXXXXX	Unverified Account
ACCOUNT NAME	XXXXXXXXXX	Unverified Account

Debt validation includes the following:

1. Who was the original creditor on this account, and what was the account number?
2. What was the original amount owed? Please provide a complete payment history, starting with the original creditor.
3. Please provide me documentation that clearly outlines an agreement to pay this amount of money to the creditor with an original signature.
4. What was the first date of delinquency for this account?
5. I would like a copy of any agreement that gives you the rights to collect on this unproven debt, or "proof of acquisition by assignment."
6. I would like the total amount that you paid for this account and/ or how the total amount owed was calculated.

Again, I require full compliance with the requests outlined in this letter within 30 days of your certified receipt of the letter, or a complete removal from my credit profile, in writing, of your findings. In the event that you do not comply with my request, I reserve the right exhaust all consumer rights extended to me, file a complaint with the FTC, and appropriate county, state, and federal agencies. I also hereby maintain my right to take private civil action against your company to recover any damages incurred as a result of your non-compliance.

Sincerely,

YOUR NAME

[Enclosures]

[DATE]

FULL NAME
ADDRESS
ADDRESS
SSN

CREDIT BUREAU
ADDRESS
ADDRESS

RE: VALIDATION OF ACCOUNTS- SECOND REQUEST

To Whom It May Concern:

The unverified items listed below remain on my credit report in violation of federal law. Despite my request for an investigation with proof of documentation, you stated [WHAT WAS STATED], but you did not provide the proof requested. As it stands, there is no information as to who verified these accounts. You are required under the FCRA to have a copy of the original creditor's documentation with my signature on it on file to verity this information is mine and is correct.

Again, I neither affirm, nor deny any purported debt you claim I owe to the listed companies.

This letter is being sent to you in response to an entry made on my credit report. Please be advised that this is not a refusal to pay the debt, but a notice sent pursuant to the Fair Debt Collection Practices Act, that your claim that I owe you money is being disputed, and validation is requested for the alleged debts listed.

Under the Fair Credit Reporting Act, I have the right to request validation of the debt being reported as owed, charged off, in collections, or any other remark in kind. Please regard this as a formal request for the physical verification of the original signed consumer contract for any and all accounts I request to be investigated that you post on my credit report. If this information is not furnished, it is possible that anyone paying to furnish data could be sending in my information fraudulently.

This is a request for proof that I am the right person and that there is a documented contractual obligation which is binding on me to the account being reported. Please note, this is NOT a request for "verification" via E-Oscar or proof of my mailing address, but a request for VALIDATION made per the Fair Debt Collection Practices Act. Proof is quantified by an original Consumer Contract with my Signature on it. Your inability to produce this information could affect my ability to obtain credit.

Reporting inaccurate and unsubstantiated information to a credit reporting agency may constitute as fraud under federal law (FCRA). Compliance with this request is required per the laws of my state and per federal laws that all unverifiable accounts must be removed and if you are unable to provide me a copy of verifiable proof, you must remove the accounts listed below:

Account	Account Number	Provide Physical Verification
ACCOUNT NAME	XXXXXXXXX	Unverified Account
ACCOUNT NAME	XXXXXXXXXX	Unverified Account

Debt validation includes the following:

1. Who was the original creditor on this account, and what was the account number?
2. What was the original amount owed? Please provide a complete payment history, starting with the original creditor.
3. Please provide me documentation that clearly outlines an agreement to pay this amount of money to the creditor with an original signature.
4. What was the first date of delinquency for this account?
5. I would like a copy of any agreement that gives you the rights to collect on this unproven debt, or "proof of acquisition by assignment."
6. I would like the total amount that you paid for this account and/ or how the total amount owed was calculated.

Again, I require full compliance with the requests outlined in this letter within 30 days of your certified receipt of the letter, or a complete removal from my credit profile, in writing, of your findings. In the event that you do not comply with my request, I reserve the right exhaust all consumer rights extended to me, file a complaint with the FTC, and appropriate county, state, and federal agencies. I also hereby maintain my right to take private civil action against your company to recover any damages incurred as a result of your non-compliance.

Sincerely,

YOUR NAME

[Enclosures]

Dispute Letter #3

[DATE]

FULL NAME
ADDRESS
ADDRESS
SSN

CREDIT BUREAU
ADDRESS
ADDRESS

RE: VALIDATION OF ACCOUNTS

To Whom It May Concern:

Please regard this letter as my third written request. I can and will fully exercise my rights to pursue litigation as a consumer per the FCRA. If this is not resolved, I can pursue relief for all monetary damages that I may be entitled to me per the FCRA regarding your continued willful and negligent non-compliance.

The unverified items listed below remain on my credit report in violation of federal law. Despite my request for an investigation with proof of documentation, you stated [WHAT WAS STATED], but you did not provide the proof requested. As it stands, there is no information as to who verified these accounts. You are required under the FCRA to have a copy of the original creditor's documentation with my signature on it on file to verity this information is mine and is correct.

Again, I neither affirm, nor deny any purported debt you claim I owe to the listed companies.

This letter is being sent to you in response to an entry made on my credit report. Please be advised that this is not a refusal to pay the debt, but a notice sent pursuant to the Fair Debt Collection Practices Act, that your claim that I owe you money is being disputed, and validation is requested for the alleged debts listed.

Under the Fair Credit Reporting Act, I have the right to request validation of the debt being reported as owed, charged off, in collections, or any other remark in kind. Please regard this as a formal request for the physical verification of the original signed consumer contract for any and all accounts I request to be investigated that you posted on my credit report. If this information is not furnished, it is possible that anyone paying to furnish data could be sending in my information fraudulently.

This is a request for proof that I am the right person and that there is a documented contractual obligation which is binding on me to the account being reported. Please note, this is NOT a request for "verification" via E-Oscar or proof of my mailing address, but a request for VALIDATION made per the Fair Debt Collection Practices Act. Proof is quantified by an original Consumer Contract with my Signature on it. Your inability to produce this information could affect my ability to obtain credit.

Reporting inaccurate and unsubstantiated information to a credit reporting agency may constitute as fraud under federal law (FCRA). Compliance with this request is required per the laws of my state and per federal laws that all unverifiable accounts must be removed and if you are unable to provide me a copy of verifiable proof, you must remove the accounts listed below:

Account	Account Number	Provide Physical Verification
ACCOUNT NAME	XXXXXXXXX	Unverified Account
ACCOUNT NAME	XXXXXXXXXX	Unverified Account

Debt validation includes the following:

1. Who was the original creditor on this account, and what was the account number?
2. What was the original amount owed? Please provide a complete payment history, starting with the original creditor.
3. Please provide me documentation that clearly outlines an agreement to pay this amount of money to the creditor with an original signature.
4. What was the first date of delinquency for this account?
5. I would like a copy of any agreement that gives you the rights to collect on this unproven debt, or "proof of acquisition by assignment."
6. I would like the total amount that you paid for this account and/ or how the total amount owed was calculated.

Again, I require full compliance with the requests outlined in this letter within 30 days of your certified receipt of the letter, or a complete removal from my credit profile, in writing, of your findings. In the event that you do not comply with my request, I reserve the right exhaust all consumer rights extended to me, file a complaint with the FTC, and appropriate county, state, and federal agencies. I also hereby maintain my right to take private civil action against your company to recover any damages incurred as a result of your non-compliance.

Sincerely,

YOUR NAME

[Enclosures]

[DATE]

FULL NAME
ADDRESS
ADDRESS
SSN

CREDIT BUREAU
ADDRESS
ADDRESS

NOTICE TO FEDERAL TRADE COMMISSION

To Whom It May Concern:

Despite my attempt to amicably resolve your continued violation of the Fair Credit Reporting Act, I have notified the Federal Trade Commission regarding your refusal to delete UNVERIFED information from my consumer file.

A copy of this letter as well as copies of the four written letters sent to you previously has become part of a formal complaint to the Federal Trade Commission and shall be used as evidence in active litigation assuming you failed to comply with my request for validation of the debt.

Sincerely,

YOUR NAME

[Enclosures]

[DATE]

FULL NAME
ADDRESS
ADDRESS

CREDIT BUREAU
ADDRESS
ADDRESS

RE: Disputing Information in Credit Report

I am writing regarding the information listed on my [CREDIT BUREAU] report. This information was furnished by your company. I have made several requests with [CREDIT BUREAU], however, they have failed to successfully comply with my request for an investigation. I have escalated the matter to your organization, and I am seeking resolution of this issue.

I have listed the items I dispute on the attached copy of my credit report(s) furnished by [CREDIT BUREAU].

Account Name: Account Number:

For example, [ACCOUNT] is [INACCURATE] or [INCOMPLETE] because [DESCRIBE THE INACCURACY AND WHY IT IS INACCURATE].

I am requesting that [CREDIT BUREAU] have the item removed.

Enclosed please find copies of [LIST ENCLOSURES] accompanying my request. This is a formal request for a reinvestigation of this matter. I am also requesting that you reach out to the credit bureaus and request that the inaccurate or incomplete information be removed immediately.

Sincerely,

[Your name]

[Enclosures]

[DATE]

CREDIT BUREAU
ADDRESS
ADDRESS

RE: FAILURE TO RESPOND TO DELETION/CORRECTION LETTER

To Whom It May Concern:

On [DATE], I sent a certified letter to your company with a formal request for an investigation. A complete investigation means that you investigate, correct, and/ or remove the disputed account outlined in the letter. As of [LETTER DATE], you have not replied to my investigation request. Enclosed please find a copy of the previous letter for your review.

Per federal law you are required to investigate my dispute request within 30 days of receiving a letter from me. You are currently violating that law.

If this issue remains unaddressed, my credit will continue to be impacted and I may sustain damages. If you decide to continue ignoring my request, I will have to escalate this issue to the Federal Trade Commission and let them know you have not been compliant.

If you any need additional information, please contact me at the address below.

Thank you.

Sincerely,

YOUR NAME
ADDRESS
ADDRESS

[Enclosures]

[DATE]

CREDIT BUREAU
ADDRESS
ADDRESS

RE: ADDING INFORMATION TO CREDIT REPORT

To Whom It May Concern:

I recently reviewed my credit report and I realized that some credit accounts are being reported, but there is information missing. This is a request to add the following accounts to my credit report to complete my credit history. Please see attached correspondence from the merchant(s) that need to be updated.

Company Name   Merchant #   Account #

Once these corrections have been made, please mail me an updated copy of my credit report. As you know, there should not be a charge for this new report.

If you need more information, please contact me at the address below.

Sincerely,

YOUR NAME
ADDRESS
ADDRESS

[Enclosures]

127

[DATE]

CREDIT BUREAU
ADDRESS
ADDRESS

RE: UNAUTHORIZED INQUIRY

To Whom It May Concern:

I recently reviewed my credit report and I realized that [COMPANY NAME] ran an unauthorized credit inquiry on me on [DATE].

I never authorized [COMPANY NAME] to take these actions and this is a blatant violation of my rights under the Fair Credit Reporting Act. This also a violation of my consumer rights to privacy. Please contact [COMPANY NAME] and please investigate the inquires.

Once these corrections have been made, please mail me an updated copy of my credit report. As you know, there should not be a charge for this new report.

If you need more information, please contact me at the address below.

Thank you.

Sincerely,

YOUR NAME
ADDRESS
ADDRESS

[Enclosures]

[DATE]

CREDIT BUREAU
ADDRESS
ADDRESS

RE: FRIVOLOUS LETTER NOTICE

To Whom It May Concern:

My request for an investigation was rejected by [CREDIT BUREAU]. In your letter, you stated that the accounts referenced in my dispute were "irrelevant and frivolous." It is unfortunate that [CREDIT BUREAU] would resort to such a deliberate stall tactic. This is a formal request to reinvestigate my credit report.

Enclosed please find a copy of my previous letter and credit report with the disputed items that need to be addressed. If you continue to engage in these stall tactics, I will report [CREDIT BUREAU] to the Federal Trade Commission.

If you have any questions, please contact me at the address below.

Thank you.

Sincerely,

YOUR NAME
ADDRESS
ADDRESS

[Enclosures]

[DATE]

CREDIT BUREAU
ADDRESS
ADDRESS

RE: **CONSUMER STATEMENT ADDITION**

To Whom It May Concern:

Since you reinvestigated my credit report, there has not been a resolution to the accuracy of my credit report. Per the FCRA, it is my right to add a statement to my credit report that will inform future creditors about the dispute

[STATEMENT: 100 WORDS OR LESS]

Once the statement(s) have been added, I need you to mail me an updated copy of my credit report. As you know, there should not be a charge for this new report.

If you need additional information, please contact me at the address below.

Thank you.

Sincerely,

YOUR NAME
ADDRESS
ADDRESS

[Enclosures]

[DATE]

CREDIT BUREAU
ADDRESS
ADDRESS

RE: BANKRUPTCY REPORTS INCOMPLETE

To Whom It May Concern:

I recently reviewed my credit report and the accounts listed below were entered in my bankruptcy but are not reported on my credit report. Enclosed please find a copy of the credit report with corresponding item numbers written next to the incorrect entries and a copy of my court records that list the credits that should be included in the bankruptcy file.

According to the Fair Credit Reporting Act, these disputed items must be updated to correctly reflect the discharge of my bankruptcy.

Once the corrections have been made, I need you to mail me updated copy of my credit report. As you know, there should not be a charge for this new report.

If you need additional information, please contact me at the address below.

Thank you.

Sincerely,

YOUR NAME
ADDRESS
ADDRESS

[Enclosures]

[DATE]

CREDIT BUREAU
ADDRESS
ADDRESS

RE: REQUEST TO UPDATE FOR COMPLETENESS OF ACCOUNT HISTORY

To Whom It May Concern:

I recently reviewed my credit report and upon viewing I noticed errors being reported in my payment history. Due to these errors, this is a request for you investigate the errors and the correct payment history to my credit report. Continuing to report inaccurate or incomplete payment history is an FCRA violation.

Incomplete Accounts:

Once the corrections have been made, I need you to mail me an updated copy of my credit report. As you know, there should not be a charge for this new report.

If you need additional information, please contact me at the address below.

Thank you.

Sincerely,

YOUR NAME
ADDRESS
ADDRESS

[Enclosures]

[DATE]

CREDIT BUREAU
ADDRESS
ADDRESS

RE: REMOVAL FROM MAILING LIST

To Whom It May Concern:

Please regard this as a formal request to have my identifying information such as my name, address, telephone number, credit report, or other information sold, furnished, shared, exchanged, with any marketers or third-party advertisers removed. Additionally, cease all credit issues from being able to prescreen my credit report with the intention of sending credit card offers.

I would like that all of my personal information stays private.

Thank you for your help.

Sincerely,

YOUR NAME
ADDRESS
ADDRESS

[Enclosures]

DATE]

CREDITOR
ADDRESS
ADDRESS

**RE: REPAYMENT AGREEMENT FOR ACCOUNT
#_____**

Dear [CREDITOR]:

Thank you for taking the time to speak with me on [DATE] regarding account number_____. As mentioned, I have paid on time in the past, however, my finances changed, and I was late for the following reason(s):

This is a request to alter our repayment agreement until my financial circumstances improve. The new amount that is manageable for me is $[AMOUNT] for [NUMBER] payment periods. After that, I anticipate I can resume making payments in full.

I would like to clarify that during this time, I won't be accessing my credit accounts with [COMPANY NAME].

If my circumstances were to change ahead of time, I will contact you immediately to make the appropriate changes.

Thank you for your understanding and help with this matter. If you need additional information, please contact me at the address below.

Sincerely,

YOUR NAME
ADDRESS
ADDRESS

[Enclosures]

[DATE]

CREDITOR
ADDRESS
ADDRESS

RE: NOTICE OF OVERDUE ACCOUNT

Dear [CREDITOR]:

Account number _____ is currently past due and I am aware of this. My
inability to make payments on time has been hindered for the following reasons:

```
┌─────────────────────────────────────────────────────────┐
│                                                           │
│                                                           │
└─────────────────────────────────────────────────────────┘
```

I do not anticipate having these financial challenges long term. I would like to
temporarily suspend payments and resume them on [DATE]. During this
adjustment time, I am requesting that my payments are not reported as late to the
credit bureaus.

Thank you in advance for your help. Your collaboration is greatly appreciated.

If you need additional information, please contact me at the address below.

Sincerely,

YOUR NAME
ADDRESS
ADDRESS

[Enclosures]

[DATE]

CREDITOR
ADDRESS
ADDRESS

RE: DECREASED PAYMENT REQUEST

Dear [CREDITOR]:

I am currently having some financial challenges and ability to make payments on time has been hindered for the following reasons:

I have looked into what I can afford to pay to each creditor at this time and created a plan to reduce my payments to $[AMOUNT].

Please regard this as request to accept my decreased payment proposal until my financial circumstance improves. This request is temporary, and I anticipate being able to resume my full monthly payment as of [DATE].

I would like to maintain the relationship I have with [CREDITOR] and do not want to compromise the trust that we have built. This is an effort to uphold our relationship while also ensuring I do not face hardships. Lastly, while I am faced with these challenges, I will not be accessing any of the credit available to me until I can resume full payments.

Assuming my request is approved, I will remit my first reduced payment.

Thank you for your cooperation during this period of financial difficulty.

If you need additional information, please contact me at address below.

Sincerely,

YOUR NAME
ADDRESS
ADDRESS

[Enclosures]

[DATE]

Federal Trade Commission
Consumer Response Center
600 Pennsylvania Ave., NW
Washington, DC 20580

RE: [CREDIT BUREAU/CREDITOR] COMPLAINT LETTER

To Whom It May Concern:

I am writing to file a complaint against [CREDIT BUREAU/CREDITOR].

Offer an explanation and a detailed account of who you've spoken to, the
phone number you called, the date you called, and the result of this
conversation.

Over the past few months, I've made several attempts to resolve this issue;
however, I have not been successful. Enclosed are the documents that support my
dealings with [CREDIT BUREAU/CREDITOR].

I am requesting your assistance in resolving this issue. If you need additional
information, please contact me at the address below.

Sincerely,

YOUR NAME
ADDRESS
ADDRESS

[Enclosures]

137

[DATE]

CREDIT BUREAU
ADDRESS
ADDRESS

RE: CREDIT FREEZE

Dear [CREDIT BUREAU]:

This is a request you conduct a credit freeze on my credit file.

My name is _____

My former name was _____

My current address is listed below_____

My former address was (two former addresses) _____

My social security number is _____

My date of birth is _____

I have enclosed photocopies of my state-issued identification along with proof of current residence. (Attach a utility bill issued within the last 30 days).

Or

I have experienced identity theft and have attached a copy of the policy report from my local police station. As you know, my consumer rights in [STATE] allows me to have a free credit freeze.

Thank you in advance for honoring my request.

Sincerely,

YOUR NAME
ADDRESS
ADDRESS

[Enclosures]

[DATE]

FULL NAME
ADDRESS
ADDRESS

Advanced Resolution Services, Inc.
5005 Rockside Road Suite 600
Independence, OH 44131

ATTN: SECURITY FREEZE DEPARTMENT

To Whom It May Concern:

Please accept this letter as my formal request to place a security freeze on my account.

I know that I will need to prove my identity, so please see my identifying information below:

FULL NAME:
ADDRESS:
PHONE NUMBER:
SOCIAL SECURITY NUMBER:
D.O.B:
EMAIL:
REQUEST: Opt-Out

After you have honored this request, I expect a written confirmation notice mailed to the address listed above.
Enclosed you will find my driver's license, utility bill, and a copy of my Social Security card to confirm my identity and safeguard the expedited processing my request.

Sincerely,

YOUR NAME
ADDRESS
ADDRESS

[Enclosures]

[DATE]

FULL NAME
ADDRESS
ADDRESS

Innovis
P.O. Box 495
Pittsburgh, PA 145230-1689

ATTN: SECURITY FREEZE DEPARTMENT

To Whom It May Concern:

Please accept this letter as my formal request to remove my name permanently from the lists that your company provides to businesses that send firm (preapproved/prescreened) offers of credit or insurance. Under the federal law, you are required to comply.

I know that your company will need some sort of verification to prove my identity. My information is clearly shown below:

FULL NAME:
ADDRESS:
PHONE NUMBER:
SOCIAL SECURITY NUMBER:
D.O.B:
EMAIL:
REQUEST: Opt-Out

After you have honored this request, I expect a written confirmation notice mailed to the address listed above.

Enclosed you will find my driver's license, utility bill, and a copy of my Social Security card to confirm my identity and safeguard the expedited processing my request.

Sincerely,

YOUR NAME
ADDRESS
ADDRESS

[Enclosures]

DATE]

FULL NAME
ADDRESS
ADDRESS

Security Freeze
Exchange Service Center –NCTUE P.O. Box 105561
Atlanta, GA 30348

ATTN: SECURITY FREEZE DEPARTMENT

To Whom It May Concern:

Please accept this letter as my formal request to place a security freeze on my
account.

I know that I will need to prove my identity, so please see my identifying
information below.

FULL NAME:
ADDRESS:
PHONE NUMBER:
SOCIAL SECURITY NUMBER:
D.O.B:
EMAIL:
REQUEST: Opt-Out

After you have honored this request, I expect a written confirmation notice mailed
to the address listed above.

Enclosed you will find my driver's license, utility bill, and a copy of my Social
Security card to confirm my identity and safeguard the expedited processing my
request.

Sincerely,

YOUR NAME
ADDRESS
ADDRESS

[Enclosures]

[DATE]

FULL NAME
ADDRESS
ADDRESS

SageStream, LLC Consumer Office,
P.O. Box 503793
San Diego, CA 92150

ATTN: OPT OUT DEPARTMENT
      RE: 5 YEAR OPT-OUT

To Whom It May Concern:

Please accept this letter as my formal request to place a security freeze on my account.

I know that I will need to prove my identity, so please see my identifying information below.

FULL NAME:
ADDRESS:
PHONE NUMBER:
SOCIAL SECURITY NUMBER:
D.O.B:
EMAIL:
REQUEST: Opt-Out

After you have honored this request, I expect a written confirmation notice mailed to the address listed above.

Enclosed you will find my driver's license, utility bill, and a copy of my Social Security card to confirm my identity and safeguard the expedited processing my request.

Sincerely,

YOUR NAME
ADDRESS
ADDRESS

[Enclosures]

[DATE]

FULL NAME
ADDRESS
ADDRESS

TELECHECK SERVICES, INC (hereinafter "Company")
P.O.BOX 6806
HAGERSTOWN, MD 21741

ATTN: OPTOUT DEPARTMENT

To Whom It May Concern:

Please accept this letter as my formal request to place a security freeze on my account.

I know that I will need to prove my identity, so please see my identifying information below.

FULL NAME:
ADDRESS:
PHONE NUMBER:
SOCIAL SECURITY NUMBER:
D.O.B:
EMAIL:
REQUEST: Opt-Out

After you have honored this request, I expect a written confirmation notice mailed to the address listed above.

Enclosed you will find my driver's license, utility bill, and a copy of my Social Security card to confirm my identity and safeguard the expedited processing my request.

Sincerely,

YOUR NAME
ADDRESS
ADDRESS

[Enclosures]

YOUR FULL NAME
ADDRESS
ADDRESS

DATE

COMPANY NAME
ADDRESS
ADDRESS

RE: Account # _____

This is in response to communication regarding [COMPANY NAME] account on [DATE] over the phone.

It is my desire to satisfy the alleged debt for the **total** amount of $[AGREEMENT AMOUNT]. I have enclosed [FORM OF PAYMENT] [PAYMENT ID #] that fulfills this settlement agreement.

Under the Fair Debt Collection Practices Act, you are required to update my information with each of the credit bureaus you report to and inform each bureau that you are no longer able to collect on the alleged amount owed.

Furthermore more, please regard this letter as a statement that I wish for this collection account to no longer appear on my credit report. Processing payment of [FORM OF PAYMENT] [PAYMENT ID #] as the settled amount is an acknowledgement of this agreement, and it is expected that this information will be made clear to all bureaus being reported to, in order to remove this account from my credit report. If this agreement cannot be honored by your organization, please return the check to the address listed above.

Should you continue to attempt to collect this debt after this payment is processed and our agreement is complete, I reserved the right to pursue litigation. I am a litigious citizen and I reserve the right to sue your organization in Small Claims Court and subject you to a fine of $1000 per violation, as well as my attorney fees, and court costs and any other damages I sustain because of your noncompliance.

Additionally, I would like to remind you that you are legally obligated not to report a debt that has not been properly validated or is already settled as in this case- assuming you process the [FORM OF PAYMENT] [PAYMENT ID #].

www.ingramcontent.com/pod-product-compliance
Lightning Source LLC
Chambersburg PA
CBHW060805100426

42813CB00004B/957

has branded herself as a personal finance innovator through the content shared on and offline.

Nathalie has, almost naturally, delivered the blueprint for improving credit and personal finances. Her growing fan base travel in droves towards the content she shares, and their loyalty is definite.

About The Author

Nathalie Noisette

Nathalie Noisette is the credit "secret weapon." As the strategic force behind her company, Credit Conversion, Nathalie is responsible for curating a unique customer experience that allows consumers insights to transform their credit and personal finances. Credit Conversion has received an award from Best Company as an "Expert Contributor" in finance and media mentions in countless major online publications such as Yahoo Finance, MSN Money, and Business Insider.

Nathalie is a leading expert, speaker, and published author on credit and personal finance. Nathalie has also published several children's books about personal finance that assist parents in introducing financial concepts as early as three years old.

Nathalie has been responsible for designing intricate credit improvement strategies and devising accelerated interest-eliminating plans for over eight years.

Instinctively, Noisette's passion for educating consumers lead her to construct the business Credit Conversion that has gained a cult-like following of individuals looking to transition their credit, money mindset, and personal finances. Noisette's influence remains a constant through her podcast "Mental Money," centered around shifting the listener's relationship with money. Each podcast episode invites the listener to access the lesser publicized conversations and ideas experts have about money. The podcast garners thousands of listeners per episode. Noisette

I am sure you wish to resolve this matter as quickly as possible and avoid any unnecessary complications. Should you fail to respond to this letter within 30 business days, I will not hesitate to report these violations my State's Attorney General, the Federal Trade Commission, and file a complaint with the Better Business Bureau.

Sincerely,

[YOUR NAME]